WARBURG MODELS

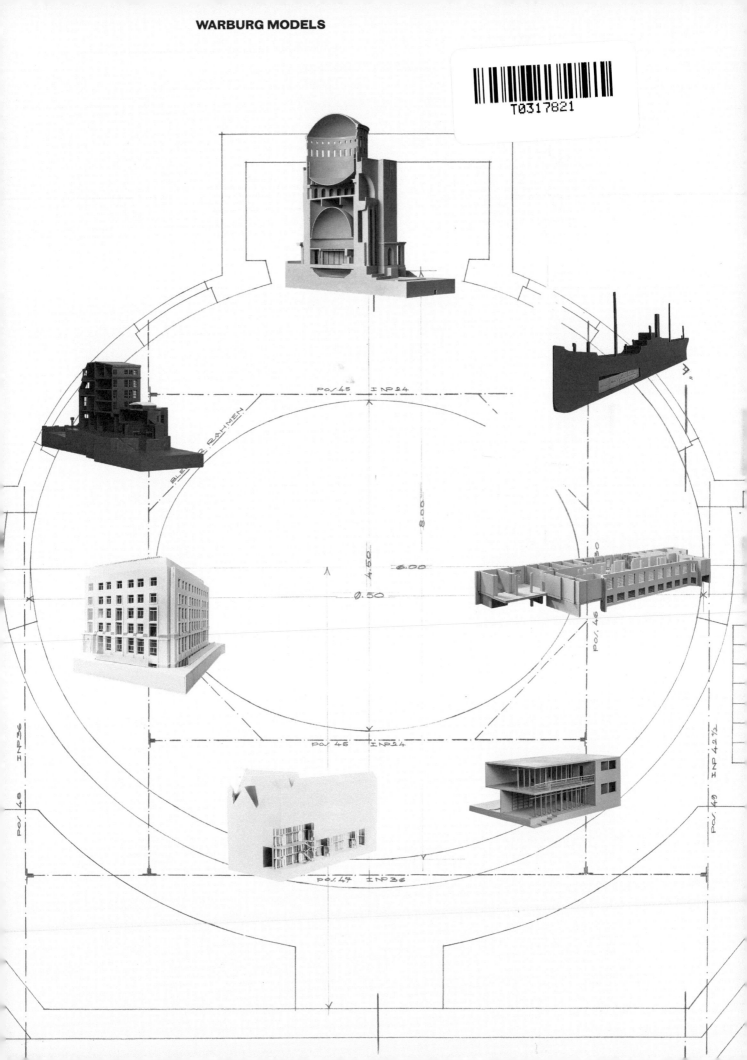

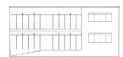

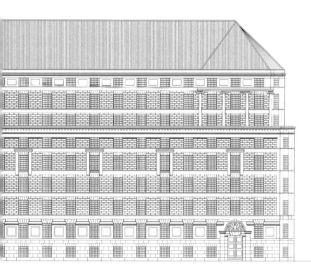

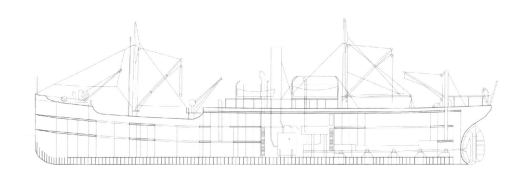

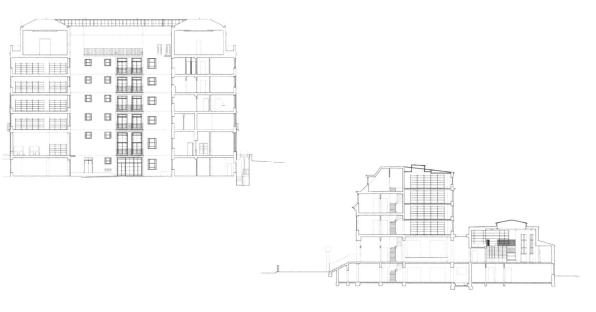

Tim Anstey and Mari Lending

WARBURG MODELS
Buildings as
Bilderfahrzeuge

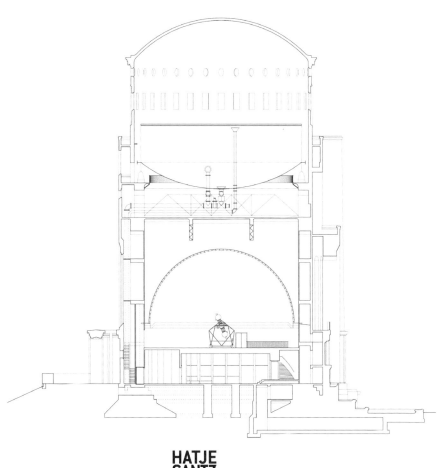

HATJE
CANTZ

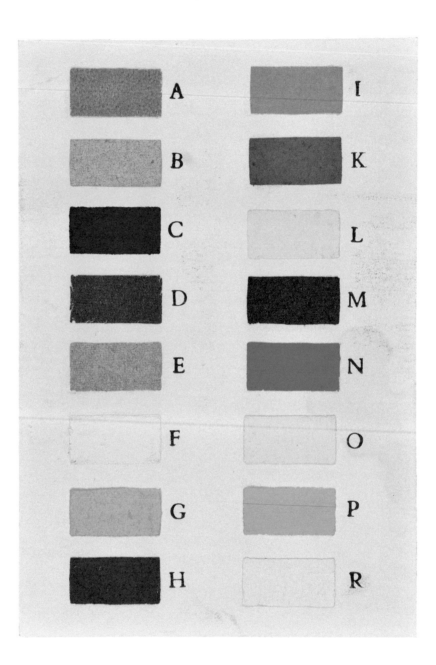

Colour chart for coding
book spines, in use at
the Warburg Library from
1922 to 1981.

Stack Room, "Art History" (main level),
"Topography, Applied Arts" (mezzanine).
Warburg Institute, Imperial Institute
Buildings, ca. 1952.

WARBURG MODELS
Tim Anstey and Mari Lending

At the start of the twentieth century the German art historian Aby Warburg saw a connection between the circulation of images, the emotive power of physical movement, and the development of material cultural production. Warburg was very much a child of the circulatory nineteenth century, of its obsession with movement and its saturation by media. As an errant member of a powerful banking family, he inherited a banker's interest in questions of circulation and a capacity for identifying new contexts where investment might lead to unexpected profit. Where his four brothers concerned themselves with maintaining the position of the family business (Max Warburg became chairman and Fritz acted as a director of M. M. Warburg & Co. in Hamburg) and with developing family and international financial ties in the United States (Paul Warburg's expertise lay behind the establishment of the American Federal Reserve, and Felix married into the Loeb banking family and became managing partner of the New York house of Kuhn, Loeb & Co.), the eldest brother Aby's concerns were with cultural capital. The markets he exploited provided new kinds of evidence about the past, particularly about the relationship between Eurasian antiquity and the European Renaissance, reappraising the survival of ancient traits in the cultural production of later epochs. Warburg's contribution to the history of art is undoubted. The frameworks for cultural interpretation evolved within the institute he founded in 1921 to develop *Kulturwissenschaft* (cultural science) retain their relevance today.

In trying to make sense of the past and in interpreting what was at stake in the production of visual art through history, Warburg and his collaborators became sensitive to the material lives of images; that is to say, to the biographies of material artifacts that carried representations (books, prints, paintings; sometimes tapestries or domestic furnishings) from one place to another. He called these phenomena *Bilderfahrzeuge*—"image-vehicles"—capturing in an elegant way the combination of imaginary association and material construction that his idea of cultural transference implied. This style of thought made it possible to plot "flows" of cultural information across time and space, explaining the transfer of visual imagery and shifting, interpretive associations. It also highlighted a connection between the motive and the emotive quality of travelling images. Warburg was interested in how antique representations of movement and force, textual and visual, would recur in later artistic expression, attributing a special potency to representations that, in whatever way, signalled action through frozen movement. Such examples of the vivid afterlives of ancient *Pathosformeln* were powerfully explored in his studies of antique imagery in fifteenth-century Florentine painting, exemplified through a series of iconic female figures: a nymph bearing a basket in Ghirlandaio's *Birth of St. John the Baptist* or Botticelli's figurations in the *Primavera* and the *Birth of Venus*. In all of them motion and emotion were joined.

1 Aby Warburg in Arizona, April 1896.

2 Reading/lecture room, KBW. Photographic album, 1926.

A principal tool for tracking the kind of gossamer connections on which this view of cultural history relied was a book collection whose organization could be moulded and redistributed to bring out hidden alignments. Warburg's library was a device for such spatial tracking, and it had, from its first inception, a spatial dimension that was unusual. Perhaps inevitably, this spatial aspect became, as Warburg's enquiries were formalized and the book collection expanded, an architectural one. An attention to the way spatial trajectories had generated influence across wide swathes of history—on how *Bilderfahrzeuge* travelled—produced a concordant concern with the way the library itself was spatialized, and on how movement was implied in its organization, fostered through sequences and juxtapositions.

Warburg's itinerant library, its captivating idiosyncrasies and radical relational order, have proven enduring objects of fascination across disciplines. In all this work the special character of the institution's architectural spaces has been tacitly admitted, but never consistently studied as a whole. *Warburg Models: Buildings as Bilderfahrzeuge* focuses on a highly pragmatic and physical dimension of the library's history: the built spaces that have housed the holdings, their disparate manifestations in their motive and emotive aspects, and the necessary reinscription of this architecture at various addresses. By unearthing drawings (spanning from sketches to annotated technical drawings), letters, and accounts of these architectural projects in the archives of the Warburg Institute and the collections of the Royal Institute of British Architects, and by triangulating our observations with the archival work already carried out on a few of the buildings (particularly that of Tilmann von Stockhausen, Uwe Fleckner, and Elizabeth Sears on the Kulturwissenschaftliche Bibliothek Warburg, the Planetarium in Hamburg, and the Warburg Institute's premises in London), we hope to provide yet another fragment to sustain the afterlife of a cornucopian tradition of ideas. In our case, a century's worth of images and texts, that throw light on built and unbuilt projects, have also been transformed in the sense that we have translated this highly modern, even avant-garde, architectural trajectory into three dimensions. Introducing the scale model as a vehicle to understand the concerns of an architecture that might be called "Warburgian," we attempt to construct a "little library"—a visualization of buildings and a retelling of their stories organized according to an overarching principle of architectural representation—revealing connections through juxtaposition and sequence in a way that recalls the efficacies of Warburg's own instrumentalizing library.

"From floor to ceiling the walls were covered in books, the pantry became a stack room, heavy shelves were hanging dangerously over doors, the billiard room had been changed into an office, in the hall, on the landings, in the drawing-room of the family—everywhere books, books, books; and new books came in every day."[1]

In 1943, Fritz Saxl, the acting director of the library from 1920 to 1924, and formal director from Warburg's death in 1929 until his own in 1948, recalled his mentor and colleague's book collection as it threatened to consume Warburg's home at Heilwigstrasse 114 in the suburbs of Hamburg. Saxl first encountered the collection in 1910. "Bewildered" by the sight of the 15,000 volumes in their "baffling" arrangement, observing the collector who "never tired of shifting and re-shifting them," and alert to the constant regrouping of a collection whose ever-changing order was based on Warburg's credo "the law of the good neighbour," he was struck by how the deluge of books and documents appeared to be "intensely alive."[2] In the early 1920s, embarking on the endeavour of "developing this manifestly personal creation into a public institution," Saxl and Gertrud Bing—recruited to the staff in Hamburg from December 1921, and later the Institute's assistant director and then director from 1955 until 1959—attempted "to 'normalize'" the order of the, by then, 20,000 volumes without destroying "the original character of the collection as an instrument for research."[3] Together, Saxl and Bing laid the ground for a hypermodern organization in this rare book collection. Following a long (and much discussed) mental breakdown, Warburg returned to Hamburg from Ludwig Binswanger's private clinic at Bellevue in Kreuzlingen, Switzerland, in August 1924. On May 1, 1926, the purpose-built Kulturwissenschaftliche Bibliothek Warburg (KBW) was formally inaugurated on the plot at Heilwigstrasse 116, adjacent to Warburg's own home and interconnected with it (they shared a lift). "Built with economy of space like a ship, and equipped with modern library equipment," the new building was articulated externally on the model of the town houses adjacent to it. Together, Heilwigstrasse 114 and 116 were arranged to hold 120,000 volumes.[4]

3 Sandro Botticelli, *Primavera*, ca. 1480. Uffizi Gallery, Florence.

Architecture, interiors, and technological systems played a crucial role in the way Aby Warburg and his followers conducted their interrogation of culture and memory. Between 1923 and 1958 this led to six architectural projects. The KBW was completed to the designs of a young Hamburg architect, Gerhard Langmaack, with guiding advice from the city's *Baudirektor* Fritz Schumacher, whom the Warburg family knew well. A connection to banking efficiency and an almost neurotic emphasis on internal systems of exchange were evident in this building. Architectural and bibliographic order were conditioned by industrial technologies of communication: more than twenty telephones, an epidiascope projector that could cast images from books or lantern slides across the reading room, a pneumatic tube system for moving book request slips, book lifts, and conveyor belts: all these squeezed into a building volume that remained domestic in scale. In 1927, as the members of the nascent Warburg Institute established themselves in this building, Warburg became involved in a scheme to create a permanent exhibit on the history of cosmology, together with a small library of relevant books, within the city's plans to purchase a Zeiss star-projector and set up a planetarium for Hamburg. The planetarium was to occupy a much larger structure, that of a disused brick water tower, an expressionist building designed by the Munich-based architect Oskar Menzel and constructed during World War I. Warburg and Saxl proposed to install the exhibit in two dedicated rooms in this empty shell, a plan realized, at no small expense, by Warburg's followers, who would present, by means of images and casts, an overview of historical understandings of the heavens and their relation to human destiny as manifest in cultures from ancient Babylon and Egypt to modern Europe. The exhibit opened in 1930, a year after Warburg passed away.

In 1933, when National Socialist politics threatened both its activities and its existence in Germany, Warburgs' library transferred to London. Saxl and Edgar Wind, with help from the Warburg family and an extraordinary intervention from UK academia, arranged the removal. Bing orchestrated two successive shipments of property (the KBW building would be stripped), both on the HAPAG steamship *Hermia*: the books went first, over 500 crates shipped from Hamburg on Tuesday, December 12, 1933. The *Hermia* thus provided a brief home for the library, acting as a kind of temporary image-vehicle carrying its ideas and influences. This "transplantation" happened in the conviction "that the Institute's continental roots could not fail to flourish in British soil," in the words of Eric M. Warburg, Aby's nephew, who coordinated the move for the family.[5]

In London, despite uncertainty and straitened circumstances, the pattern of architectural commissioning initiated in Hamburg continued. As the library and its scholars moved through a series of homes, they collaborated with the avant-garde architectural group

NEW PENGUIN POND

Tecton, established in 1931 by the Russian émigré architect Berthold Lubetkin together with a group of Architectural Association graduates, tying the Institute's design ambition to the boldest modernism in London: the Penguin Pool and the Gorilla House at London Zoo (1933–34), and the apartment complex Highpoint 1 (1935) were realized in the same years. Later, as they planned a permanent home, the Institute's leaders negotiated with the office of the University of London's architect, Charles Holden. Holden had become famous during the 1930s for his streamlined Underground stations, although by the time the Warburg Institute encountered him, the production of his office had moved to a very 1950s post-war abstract classicism, to the frustration of the then director Gertrud Bing.

Between 1934 and 1937, as the political outlook worsened in Europe, the Institute occupied part of the ground floor of Sir Frank Baines's monumental and newly constructed state-of-the-art offices at Thames House on Millbank, Westminster. Within this building, which became home to a variety of tenants including the British Secret Service MI5 during the same years, the Tectonite Godfrey Samuel tailored the library into an elegant, horizontal, tightly planned, modernist interior. His proposal reused much of the furniture and shelving from the library in Hamburg but changed the relationship between its spatial layout and its readers. While collaborating intimately in saving and running the Warburg Institute as director and assistant director, Saxl and Bing also commissioned from Samuel a house for a life together in the new capital. Between the summer of 1934 and January 1935, three schemes were worked out for a cottage at Bromley, leaving behind a set of seductive drawings and a detailed correspondence between the architect and the two Warburg scholars: a lost continental modernist house on a beautifully sloped plot in Elstree Hill, Bromley, about forty minutes' drive south-east of the city. The project was never

4 Penguin Pool, London
Zoo, Regents Park,
London. Postcard, ca. 1934.

realized—in 1935 Bing and Saxl feared that the Warburg Library might relocate to the United States—but many of the ideas evident in the plans were realized in Samuel's contemporary commissions, particularly that for the country house for another art historian, Ellis Waterhouse, at Overshot Hall in Oxfordshire (1935).

After a frustrating hiatus, as building works were completed, the Institute reopened to the public in February 1939 in rooms in a wing of the Imperial Institute in South Kensington, a grandiose white elephant of a building designed by Thomas Edward Collcutt, born out of an 1880s dream of making permanent an exhibition to link Britain and its Empire with Queen Victoria's Jubilee celebrations. The eerie and eclectic complex this created formed an unlikely framework for the activities of the Warburg Institute, but one which provided its London home for twenty years (apart from its evacuation during the Second World War). An American junior fellow vividly described the complex as "too gigantic in size, too fantastic in design, and too aimless in purpose for anything on the human scale," recalling that the library "was cold and dark, colder and darker than the outdoors," and that "high overhead hung a pale bulb in whose distant and faint illumination I read and took notes, often with gloved fingers."[6] Even at the Imperial Institute the Warburgians made architectural incisions, cutting a staircase through the Victorian structure to create a link between reading room and stackrooms, and creating a "bizarre atrium, set all around with office doors from which world-famous scholars would pop out and in again—like an apotheosized cuckoo-clock."[7] After 1943, various proposals were developed for a new building, for which first Fritz Saxl and finally Gertrud Bing acted as the commissioning clients. Charles Holden's design, part of the masterplan developed for the University of London, resulted in the construction of the library's present home at Woburn Square in Bloomsbury, inaugurated in 1958. As in Hamburg, "ΜΝΗΜΟΣΥΝΗ" was transcribed over the entrance—incised in stone in Hamburg, carved in wood in London—emphasizing how the Warburg scholars imprinted their new homes with institutional memory.

The arrangement of these various undertakings occupied the directors of the Warburg Institute continuously over four decades. In all the different instantiations of the library, an identity emerged between the spatial organization of the building and the intellectual organization of a set of ideas around cultural memory, projecting a tie between architectural space and intellectual order. The KBW in Hamburg divided Warburg's book collection over four floors in a reinforced concrete bunker at the centre of a masonry building, each level identified with a major theme, or "problem," for the library's research: *Bild* (first floor), *Orientierung* (second), *Wort* (third), and *Handlung* (fourth floor). In the moves the library made in London this order was both preserved and reinterpreted. At Thames House

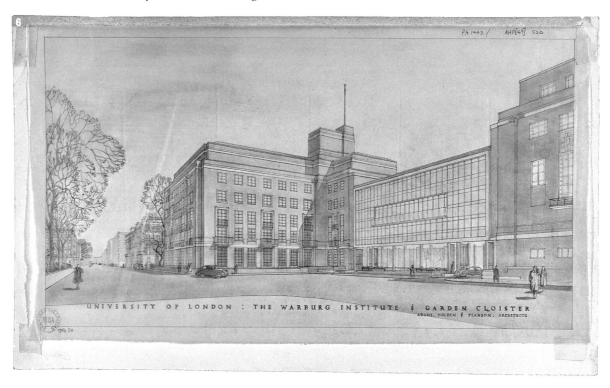

the books, laid out in a single space, were catalogued under more descriptive English section headings, moving from "Religion, Natural Science and Philosophy" (corresponding to *Orientierung*) to "Social and Political Life" (*Handlung*). At the Imperial Institute Buildings this alternative ordering was disrupted, but, after additional space was allotted in 1950, it proved possible in 1952 to reshelve the books according to a fourfold structure: "Orientation" (rooms five and four); "Word" (room three); "Image" (room two); and "Significant Act" [*Dromenon*] (room one).[8] The building that eventually became the present Warburg Institute reinscribed the vertical organization of floors corresponding to catalogue divisions as had been done in Hamburg, to arrive at a final disposition: "Image" (first floor); "Word" (second); "Orientation" (third); and "Action" (fourth floor).

In the examination of these histories of architectural commissioning, it becomes evident that the formal relationships which were reinscribed in the library layout at the various addresses the Institute occupied were part of a wider pattern, finding strong resonances in Aby Warburg's structures of thought. The scholars of the Warburg Institute "furnished" their buildings with collections of familiar objects that moved from one site to another. At the same time, they furnished them with particular nuances of meaning through rituals of translation and relocation, and through the recirculation of these objects. What results is an architecture that one could call "vehicular," in as much as the impact of these architectural projects was connected to the way in which things—image-things as well as material-things—were carried about, relocated, remounted, shifted, and re-shifted. The various formal compositions which the "intensely personal creation" that was the library took on were all linked through their position within such trajectories.

5 Thomas Edward Collcutt, Imperial Institute Buildings, South Kensington, London, inaugurated 1893.

6 Adams Holden & Pearson Architects, Perspective of the Warburg Institute, ca. 1956.

Ever translative himself—he lived for extended periods in Italy and toured the United States in 1895-96 (followed by a trip to Norway)—Warburg pursued his interests with a small group of colleagues with whom he collaborated closely. They included his wife, the artist Mary Hertz; the philosopher Ernst Cassirer (who upon his first visit to the collection in Hamburg decided either to flee from it or "to remain there a prisoner for years"[9]); the philologist Franz Boll; and particularly Fritz Saxl, whom Warburg supported as a postgraduate student and appointed in 1914 to help curate his library, and Gertrud Bing, recruited in 1921 by Saxl at the suggestion of Cassirer, co-supervisor of her dissertation. As well as organizing the Institute's activities and extending the scope of the library collection, these collaborations produced the (unfinished) *Bilderatlas Mnemosyne*, which began to distil an ecology of links that Warburg saw between images produced at separate times and in remote contexts. He used his image clusters, too, to trace the historical entanglements between superstition and ratiocination in cosmology, as part of a broad investigation into what he and his followers called "orientation," those systems of belief which orient humanity in the cosmos and that produce meaning and a sense of belonging. Both these endeavours had an architectural dimension. In the *Bilderatlas*, in panel after panel, buildings appeared, captured through black-and-white photography, as complete compositions and as a near infinite series of fragments bearing sculpture, reliefs, and inscriptions. The Warburgian focus on the problem of orientation also involved architecture directly. The systems that Warburg saw as creating cultural identity were seen expressed in buildings. This occurred both in sacred architecture—whether the Mithraea of ancient Rome or a building like that of the Old Sacristy of San Lorenzo in Florence—and in profane structures—such as the room Warburg called the *salone* at the Palazzo dell Raggione in Padua, which showed "most clearly the transformation of the spherical globe onto the wall, with the numerical and rhythmic grouping of astrological signs."[10]

To illuminate the Warburg Institute's prolonged engagement with architectural projects, we present in this book biographies of six Warburg buildings, together with hyper-detailed models of them at 1:75 scale, created by architectural students at the Oslo School of Architecture and Design within an advanced master's seminar between 2020 and 2023. To these stationary *bâtiments* we add a description and model of the SS *Hermia*, the ship that transported the Institute's physical holdings and systems of thought from Hamburg to London in the distress of December 1933.

The models highlight specific aspects of the rooms the Institute occupied and probe the contexts it moved through: the intricate sectional disposition of the KBW, the huge volume of the Planetarium, the stowage spaces of the *Hermia*, the planar geometry Godfrey Samuel imposed at Thames House, the continental atmosphere of the unbuilt cottage at Bromley, the encrustation of the Imperial Institute, and finally the overgrown doll's-house quality of the Warburg Institute at Woburn Square, with its three near-identical façades and the intense relationship it created between an isolated, esoteric interior and the profane city bustling around it. The question of what scale these models should be built to stimulated a set of conversations in our seminar that appeared to touch a common architectural aspect in the thinking of the Warburg scholars. Warburgian architecture is an architecture of the room, of arranged possessions, of the interior. But these rooms always enfold points far distant, either in a literal and pedagogic way—for example in the exhibition space of the Planetarium, where reference was made to spatial journeys of continental scale in its explanation of the history of astronomy and astrology—or through allusion and juxtaposition. The Thames House interior referred to the spaces of the lost KBW

7 Aby Warburg, *Bilderatlas Mnemosyne*, panel 79. KBW, Hamburg, 1929.

in Hamburg 600 kilometres away; the cottage designed for Saxl and Bing was designed with distant landscape views in mind. Warburgian interiors, which appear to have been always both institutional and domestic in nature, incorporated a dimension that could even be intercontinental. The articulation of Woburn Square referred both to the Institute's previous homes in Hamburg and London and to the composition of the Fogg Museum of Art at Harvard University, Cambridge, Massachusetts.[11] Somehow the models constructed in Oslo had to pay heed to this coexistence of radically different scales; they needed to combine the detail of a desk lamp with the perspective of a landscape.

At the same time, the sequenced assemblage of models aims to answer to the very Warburgian tradition of juxtaposition as a way of establishing latent connection. For Warburg and his early collaborators, in a habit that appears indebted to the thinking of Fritz Saxl, a principal tool for exploring fruitful juxtaposition was the modifying effect of black-and-white reproduction. The relational links elucidated in the *Bilderatlas Mnemosyne* relied to a great extent on this technique, which turned the coloured world into conversant grey-hued tone. The exhibition panels at the Hamburg Planetarium and those later prepared by Saxl for a series of very successful exhibitions that toured the United Kingdom in the run-up to and during the Second World War all relied on this principle, which was also built into publications such as the Institute's book of one of their wartime exhibits, *British Art and the Mediterranean* (1948), edited by Saxl and Rudolph Wittkower. In our analysis, the common scale used in the models permits juxtapositions and comparisons similar to those achieved by the use of black-and-white imagery in the *Bilderatlas Mnemosyne*.

But the Warburgian world, and the Warburg scholars' thinking about that world, was not black and white. Quite the reverse. And, in an entirely inverted approach, the Warburg Library used colour to establish the same kind of juxtapositional planes of reference that Warburg, Saxl, Panofsky, Klibansky, Wind, and Wittkower established through the use of black-and-white photography in publication. Having established an esoteric (and never to be finally frozen) signature system of letters and numbers to describe the flexible and multilayered ordering of the library, and as they spatialized this arrangement, Saxl and Bing invented a system of coloured strips that were applied to the spines of the books to provide a visual signal allowing the rapid replacement of volumes within its spaces. As the books were gathered into clusters related to a theme, their common identities would be read by the broken line of a triad of colours weaving its way across from one spine to the next. The reference sheet that the Warburgians used to identify these colours with the catalogue categories, created in the early 1920s, reads today as a startlingly modernist palette: pastel blues and umbers that might grace one of Le Corbusier's contemporary interiors; pinks and yellows that speak as much of Art Deco as of Robert Mallet-Stevens or Mies van der Rohe. Here colour forms the base for identifying links between books in the same way that its absence was used to identify links between images.

The models at the centre of our collective analysis also take on and play with this 1920s palette of Hamburg colours, thus referring to the way in which it was used both to create identity and to facilitate formal and allusional continuity. The original colour chart serves as our frontispiece. Based on archival material the models are coded with this modernist palette, used to identify themes and subjects among books in the Warburg Library in their ever-changing placement on the shelves. In adopting a single colour for each composition, certain information relating to that which is modelled is purposefully excluded. The object itself is abstracted and the models work as monochrome sculpture. This too ties back to a layer of memory at work in the Warburgian scheme.

To help us interpret the drawings and the making of the buildings, we had luxurious help from a number of leading experts. Five of them have generously shared their knowledge on fragments of this Warburgian architectural history of movement and repetition. Dr. Claudia Wedepohl, archivist of the Warburg Institute, London, considers the ellipse in the *Lese- und Vortragssaal* at the KBW in Hamburg. Professor Uwe Fleckner, director at the Warburg-Haus, Hamburg, writes on the Planetarium as a "problem-building." The Norwegian artist Dag Erik Elgin returns to the issue of movement, taking his cue from the scale model of the SS *Hermia* and Aby Warburg's figure of *The Eternal Seesaw*. Elizabeth Sears, professor at the University of Michigan, unfolds a tale of allusions to the Hamburgian past and to the ongoing work of the Institute embedded in the 1958 building at Woburn Square. Professor Bill Sherman, director of the Warburg Institute in London, describes the current remodelling that is taking place on the same site, as Charles Holden's Institute is reinvented through the Warburg Renaissance project.

This book presents the results of conversations that transpired in seminar meetings in Oslo, incorporating some of the archival material on which they were based and offering the material yields of the architectural analyses in the form of the drawings and models. Saxl talked about Aby Warburg's library as "a body of living thought."[12] Pondering the provenance of the Warburg architectures via three-dimensional models that were allowed to spring into existence on the basis of recovered archived drawings and architectural debates from the 1920s onwards, this book aims to suggest how that lively quality engendered a very particular architectural sensibility, alive to colour, to duration, and to movement.

BUILDINGS AS BILDERFAHRZEUGE

Tim Anstey

A short walk from the terraced villa that formed Aby Warburg's home in Hamburg, at Heilwigstrasse 114 in the comfortable 1890s suburb of Harvestehude, lies the S-Bahn station Kellinghusenstrasse. The railway is elevated at this point and travellers waiting for the electric trains that for the last hundred years have carried passengers to and from the city centre can still see, a little way up the shining lines, the top of a water tower, a centrepiece in the city's Stadtpark, visible above the maturing trees. Articulated like an overgrown Roman mausoleum, the water tower was commissioned between 1913 and 1915 during the early phases of the First World War. A few years after the conclusion of that traumatic conflict, the million or so bricks and hundreds of cubic metres of concrete and iron used in its construction became redundant, as Hamburg invested in better infrastructure and a single pressure zone was created for the city's water supply. In 1924 the building was decommissioned and left empty. Between 1927 and his death in 1929, Warburg was instrumental in the decision of the Hamburg City Senate to insert a planetarium into this shell. It was a radical conversion, one that would have been unthinkable, perhaps, in the pre-war years but which had a kind of resonance as Europeans addressed issues of continuity and radical change during the 1920s. Inside the rather sombre expressionist brick structure the project provided a light, domed room in which cutting-edge technologies, supplied by the Zeiss company of Jena, projected accurate, animated, and coloured depictions of the changing heavens as they wheeled over the cloudy skies of the city.

The odd triangulation produced between the town-house terrace at Heilwigstrasse, where Warburg was a resident from 1909 to 1929, the elevated railway that traversed and moved its occupants across the urban landscape, and the water tower, a remnant from a disjoined past emerging into a vibrant present, suggests many of the themes important for considering the role of architecture in the thinking of Aby Warburg and his associates. These join concerns with memory and technology, space and travel, orientation and dwelling, change and duration. The story of Warburg's involvement with the Hamburg Planetarium forms a good place to begin to understand the implications of these couplings.

Aby Warburg's interest in planetaria stemmed from a concern he shared with Fritz Saxl to understand the origins of scientific inquiry, and particularly to understand the continuities that existed between superstitious and rational systems of belief. The history of astronomy and astrology had become a test case in which to examine these tensions; a planetarium might provide a fitting context for presenting that history.[1] The strange possibility of using the redundant water tower to house such a project in Hamburg seemed to Warburg full of visionary possibility: as well as providing a high-tech, futuristic experience in which a reclining audience travelled among the stars, the building might create "a receptive mirror reflecting rearward

1 Exhibition room, *Bildersammlung zur Geschichte von Sternglaube und Sternkunde (An Image History of Astrology and Astronomy)*, Hamburg Planetarium, 1930.

looking views."[2] As a way of realizing this potential, Warburg and Saxl proposed an exhibition. It was to occupy a quadrant of a double-height ground-floor space, beneath the enormous circular domed room that was constructed to contain the planetarium proper, and presented a *Bildersammlung zur Geschichte von Sternglaube und Sternkunde*—an image history of astrology and astronomy that told the history of human cosmological thought. The idea was to present a series of stations which, viewed in sequence, explained how rational observation and superstitious belief were continuously interwoven through history. The headings that were used are a good indicator of the overlaps the designers sought to articulate: "The Arabs as Heirs to Greek Science"; "The Influence of the Orient on the Occident in the Middle Ages"; "The End of the Oriental-Medieval Tradition."[3] The exhibition showcased both the Warburgian idea of orientation— that science and magic might be seen as entwined with histories of exchange and genealogy—and the significance of images as the means by which such systems of orientation found their legitimacy. In explicit introductory panels the design charted how images and texts related to cosmological belief migrated through space and time from antiquity to the modern era, and it charted the geography of that translation, from the Near East into Europe.[4]

There was a connection between the architectural character of the room Warburg and Saxl adopted in which to stage this story, with its high niches and sparse architectural detail, and the narrative structure they adopted. Twelve of the seventeen stations in the exhibition were disposed in pairs within six deep window embrasures against the outer wall. The remaining five occupied two short sequences on the concave inner wall on each side of the doorway into the exhibition. Entrance was made from a low, artificially lit central hallway, its roof covered in a ceiling fresco depicting the stars and figurations of European astrology, which in turn was reached by a route that penetrated the water tower building laterally, running directly beneath the space of the planetarium proper. Within the exhibition, visitors swung right towards a large diptych supported by a painted inscription that summarized the exhibition theme, sited at the north-eastern end of the room. Progressing anticlockwise and swinging left, the viewer made a loop, exploring a series of didactic panels set in oppositional pairs in the niches along the northern perimeter and adjacent to each other on the inner curving wall. Light fittings, panel frames, and architectural detailing were spartan, industrial, indeed minimal. The cyclical organization, and its relation to the cyclic schemes that guided the astrological and astronomical systems presented, was clear.

This was not the first time Warburg and Saxl had encountered the interaction between an architectural organization and a cosmological scheme. Warburg's seminal 1912 lecture on "Italian Art and In-

ternational Astrology in the Palazzo Schifanoia," published in 1922, related directly to the theme.[5] Rebuilt for Borso d'Este, the Palazzo Schifanoia in Ferrara provided a *salone* suitable for the reception of ambassadors and visiting delegations within a space of display appropriate to the fifteenth-century ducal court that hosted them. The walls of this room were covered from top to bottom with a cycle of fresco paintings produced according to a single iconographical scheme during the 1470s. These were rediscovered, "under a layer of whitewash" as Warburg had it, in 1840.[6] Warburg's lecture interpreted the remaining frescoes and pointed to the influence of three discrete systems of astrological representation in the composition of the room.

In Ferrara, as at the Hamburg Planetarium, a dramatic and distinct architectural progression articulated a journey from the space of the city into the space of the interior. In order to reach the Sala dei Mesi on the first floor, a ceremonial entrance-sequence ran anticlockwise from a portal on the street façade of the palace, under the chamber itself, out through a colonnade and up an external roofed stair to an entrance at the northern corner of the room. Viewers would have swung to the left from this entrance to commence reading the cycle,

which started with Aries, the Ram, in the opposite southern corner. The extant frescoes which Warburg could observe made a series that, like the arc an embassy would pursue in approaching the Sala dei Mesi, ran anticlockwise. From left to right on the short south-east wall the months from March to May were depicted; on the long north-east side, those from June to September.

This fresco cycle, Warburg argued, presented a comparative table in which three astrological systems were harmonized to articulate the influence of the stars and planets on the fifteenth-century lives of the d'Este family and their Ferrarese subjects. Not only were the astrological signs of the European zodiacal calendar represented (Aries, Taurus, Gemini, and so on, derived ultimately from Greek astronomy), but so too was an ancient adaptation of that system, born in Egypt and evolved in India, that divided the year into thirty-six "decans"—shorter periods of ten days of time and ten degrees of astral rotation, each with its astrological significance and associated anthropomorphic figure.[7] Overarching these two, the cycle celebrated the significance of a late-antique Greco-Roman classicizing schema, which established the twelve canonical Olympian deities as sovereigns over the signs of the zodiac. Seven identified the gods associated with the seven planets—Venus, Apollo, Mercury, and so on; others included Ceres, Vulcan, and Pallas Athena, whose name Warburg cited from the influential first-century poet Manilius, who used Pallas, rather than Minerva, to denominate the Goddess of Wisdom.[8] Each panel was arranged in three architectural storeys that moved from the earthly, depicting the doings of Borso d'Este and his court at the relevant period of the year in the lowest register, through what Warburg termed "twilit regions," where "Hellenistic astral daemons hold sway," to a light heaven, spread in a thin strip around the uppermost regions of the room, in which the pagan gods returned to "their time-honoured home ... the loftier atmosphere of the Greek Olympus."[9] The system that Warburg read was thus closely bound to the architecture of the space it occupied. Warburg took the month of March as his first example. The dark sky of the first sign after the new year (March 25 was New Year's Day in Christian Europe up until the eighteenth century) is figured aptly by Aries the Ram, flanked and surmounted by personifications of three *decans*, vicarious rulers for ten days each of Aries's reign. One of these, a "wrathful black man, gripping the cord that ties his garments," provided the iconographical clue that allowed Warburg to solve the riddle of these figures' identity.[10] Below, in the earthly realm, Borso d'Este rides "cheerfully out to hunt while servants prepare vines for the growing season."[11] In the upper heaven above, the "occupations" associated with Aries are shown (lawyers and seamstresses, those who spin threads and stitch up, are associated with the garnered wool of the Ram in the springtime of the year), together with the "victory" of Pallas Athena, the pagan deity that ruled this sign in the Greco-Roman system.

The analysis of the Palazzo Schifanoia was integral to the gestation of Warburg's conception of *Bilderfahrzeuge*, the realization that cultural development could not be explained without the material transfer of images, and the shifting, associative textual interpretations they accrued, via certain kinds of physical carrier—books, manuscripts, objects, fabrics. Warburg identified not only a cast of astrological characters springing from different historical loci and jostling for position on the walls of a palazzo in fifteenth-century Ferrara, but also the vehicles, or "conveyances," by which these personages had travelled there, and even in certain cases the routes these vehicles had probably taken. The personifications of the heavens made journeys astral and earthly. Aboard their *Bilderfahrzeuge*, hidden like nuts within the shells of esoteric lapidaries and astrological treatises, or ensconced in illustrated manuscripts and printed woodcuts, Perseus, Venus, Apollo, and Pallas Athena could maintain relationships across time and space. Warburg's "black man," a derivative figure of Perseus, had travelled from Egypt to India before finding his way "probably via Persia into the Arab culture."[12] His journey "clouded still further by translation into Hebrew and thence into French" was concluded in "Pietro d'Abano's Latin version of [the *Introductorium majus* of] Abū Maʿšar," "the principal authority in medieval astrology."[13] The notion that the esoteric image-vehicles whose paths Warburg described might connect to vehicles in a more literal sense was perhaps implicit in the imagery of the uppermost tier in the fresco cycle. Here, Pallas Athena and the other Greco-Roman deities arrived not only via the *Bilderfahrzeuge* that constituted the system of exchange that transported motifs and connections from antiquity to the present, but were pictured gliding aboard festive wagons, whose character lay somewhere between the vehicular and the architectural, their fabric hangings disguising wheels and axles. Such equipages promised movement in a similar way as a tram or a carnival float, a translation—like that of the *Bilderfahrzeuge*—somewhat mysterious, in which elements both of fluidity and stasis were implicit.

3 Francesco del Cossa, Allegory depicting the astrological month of March, Palazzo Schifanoia, Ferrara, ca. 1470. Panel and detail.

At the same time, the Palazzo Schifanoia began to highlight architectural and geometrical concerns that continued to resonate through the collaborative projects undertaken by Warburg and his followers during the 1920s. It suggested a nested sequence of spatial and symbolic relationships, spanning from the intramural to the intercontinental and the extraterrestrial. It spoke at once to earthly and heavenly cartographies, reproducing cosmological adjacencies and projecting them into an architectural frame. Its ordering, which placed the months in the same anticlockwise sequence that medieval celestial maps used to place the zodiacal signs, resulted in an architectural model that held the seed of revolutionary change. While, in the Northern Hemisphere, fifteenth-century reality situated earthbound observers securely at the centre of cosmological and experiential truth, and had the heavens revolve around them, the Sala dei Mesi projected those observers into orbit—an anticlockwise rotational path within a representation of the heavens that was fixed. The heliocentric realizations of Galileo and Kepler were not far away.

There was a striking resonance between the organization of Palazzo Schifanoia according to Aby Warburg's interpretation and Warburg and Saxl's picture exhibition in the Hamburg Planetarium. Within the Warburgian scheme both contemporary exhibition and Renaissance palazzo situated images in an active space. Both exhibition and palazzo were entered midway within the loop of the explanatory cycle. Each composition asked the viewer to begin their reading at one end of the space and to progress from right to left around a room, anticlockwise. Both examples modelled cosmologies, and both used architecture in their organization. Warburg and Saxl included the analysis of the Palazzo Schifanoia in their scheme for the planetarium exhibition ("Egyptian Rulers and Gods in the Wall Paintings of an Italian Palace from 1470" runs the title for this station) and, during the planning, discussed a series of other architectures that modelled the heavens in a similar way—a Chinese Temple of Heaven; an Egyptian tomb; a Roman Mithraeum.[14]

Earlier manifestations of the planetarium exhibition had suggested twenty subject sections in its structure, and a further three significant destinations are implied in Warburg and Saxl's design beyond the seventeen stations of the wall-mounted narrative. Inside that stark white interior in the city's Stadtpark stood a set of three equally stark, black-painted boxes, each supported on minimal chrome tubular legs, each supplied with electrical power from beneath by a cloth-covered cable. Confirmation of the architectural awareness of the curators comes as one understands what these boxes did. For these are architectural models per se—mini peep-show dioramas, each offering a view into an interior that provided a cosmological scheme arranged in an architectural space in a way similar to that used in the Palazzo Schifanoia, and indeed in the exhibition as a whole. One model portrayed the tomb of Seti I in the Valley of the Kings outside Luxor;

DIE GESCHICHTE
DER HIMMELSKUNDE
ZEIGT DIE VIELFÄLTI-
GEN FORMEN
MENSCHLICHER
WELTANSICHT·
IN DÄMONENFURCHT
UND MAGIE
BEGINNEND/MUSS
DIE MENSCHHEIT
IMMER VON NEUEM
DEN WEG ZUR
ABSTRAKTEN LOGIK
DER WISSENSCHAFTLI-
CHEN BETRACHTUNG
DURCHMESSEN

←ANFANG

4 Architectural model cases in the introductory sequence of the *Bildersammlung zur Geschichte von Sternglaube und Sternkunde* (*An Image History of Astrology and Astronomy*) exhibition, Hamburg Planetarium, 1930.

one the Great Hall of the Palazzo della Ragione in Padua; one the recently excavated Mithraeum in Ostia outside Rome. In the last year of his life Warburg was emphatic about the importance of these models to his exhibition; within weeks of his death Saxl approached Fritz Schumacher for recommendations for an architect who might carry out their construction, work "which requires artistic talent and tact."[15] What resulted was a remarkable system of architectural nesting, a set of Russian dolls at shifting scales in which associations resonated. At the periphery of the city was a park. Within the park was a water tower, found as a kind of shell without a purpose, from which one could "gaze out onto the North German plain," as Warburg put it.[16] Within the water tower was established a planetarium. Within that project was a quadrant room with a display of images and objects that talked of a simultaneity between superstitious and scientific systems of belief. And at the centre of that room was a series of architectural models that provided an account of how other architectural spaces had been purposed, sometimes repurposed, for similar systems of communication in the past.

The Planetarium introduces key concerns in what appears to be a Warburgian reading of architecture, where building and architectural

Das Zeppelinluftschiff über dem Bodensee

embellishment provide a spatial frame for cosmic orientation; and where architectural models—in several senses—take on significance in this creation. What then of the railway and the house with which I began? Why link transport infrastructure and dwelling together with this focus on orientation in a theorization of a Warburgian architectural imaginary?

In his lecture on the Palazzo Schifanoia, referring to the ways in which cultural influence travelled in the field of astrology, Warburg noted how "figures from Greek myth assumed the mystic powers of astral daemons ... all the more readily by availing themselves of the rapid conveyances supplied by that Northern invention, the art of printing."[17] This metaphor had strong contemporary resonance during the period that developed transcontinental railway, steamer, and even global air travel. Rapid conveyances, often of northern provenance, were a feature of the world Aby Warburg inhabited. The Warburg family were intimately connected with the ownership of Hamburg-Amerikanischen Packetfahrt (HAPAG), the shipping line that connected Hamburg and New York, and transferred using their ships between mansions on the Upper East Side in Manhattan and a leafy summer villa overlooking the Elbe. The first Compagnie Internationale des Wagons-Lits "Orient Express" train ran direct from Paris to Constantinople on June 1, 1889, while Warburg contemplated "Filippino Lippi's hypernervous mobility" during his first trip to Florence.[18] Its services reached Baghdad by 1930, when the Hamburg Planetarium opened. Warburg travelled (for free, sponsored by the directors of the railroad) from Baltimore to New Mexico in 1895-96 on an expedition to see the lands of the Pueblo Indians, and regularly between Hamburg, Florence, and Rome after 1890. A long period of illness kept him at the Bellevue Sanatorium in Kreuzlingen, Switzerland, from 1921 to 1924, on the shores of Lake Constance, where the Zeppelin company tested their monumental airships over waters stormy or still (their most successful machine was named *Bodensee* after the lake). As he recovered, his doctor, the eminent psychiatrist Ludwig Binswanger, found him "taking care of the details of his departure (saloon car)."[19] He travelled home to Hamburg like a head of state in his own private railway carriage, with a retinue of sanatorium staff, one of whom, Franz Alber, metamorphosed under Warburgian influence into a personal assistant, chaperone, and general factotum. Such journeys and the vehicles that made them combined carriage and image. The experience of them wormed its way deep into Warburg's history of "Contemporary Life in Motion," as the title to Panel 28-29 of the *Bilderatlas Mnemosyne*, prepared during the years of planning the Planetarium exhibition, had it. Recording geographies from Baghdad in ancient Eurasia to London, Paris, or Hamburg in modern Europe, the maps that were drawn up in the Institute to record the routes along which influences travelled from the past mirrored contemporary railway guides

5 Zeppelin *Bodensee* over Lake Constance. Postcard, ca. 1925.

6 Aby Warburg, The House on Wheels. Photographed in Pasadena, 1895.

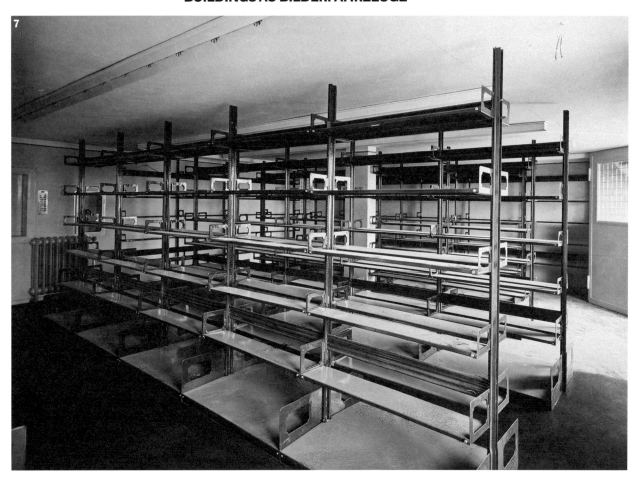

7

that charted how journeys could be made in the opposite direction. Images of vehicles—from ocean liners to Zeppelin airships—entered into the plates of the *Bilderatlas* (Panels C and 77/79 in the recently reconstructed version). Zeppelins became something of an obsession. The *salone* of the Palazzo della Ragione in Padua was "the size of an airship hangar"; an essay analysing the contents of two fifteenth-century tapestries that celebrated the deeds of Alexander the Great was titled "Airship and Submarine in the Medieval Imagination" (1913).[20] Thus, for any analysis of a Warburgian architecture, the notion of "carriage" is central. The S-Bahn railway in Hamburg, that wends its way from city centre to periphery, and which was con-structed during the same years in which Warburg, his wife Mary, and Fritz Saxl began to trace out the meandering routes taken by image-ideas from the past on their way to the present, might stand for this principle of displacement and connection. Indeed, the rail-way reifies rather precisely the architectural implications of this idea: that one cannot have *Bilderfahrzeuge* without an infrastructure of stations, tracks, and staging posts to support them. Occupying the railway carriage is an act as much architectural as anything else.

Warburg's identification of interiors such as that of the Palazzo Schifanoia or the *salone* of the Palazzo della Ragione in Padua as "immense folio pages" projected a direct connection between the notion of a building and the notion of *Bilderfahrzeuge*.[21] Buildings, in this reading, become another material support through which

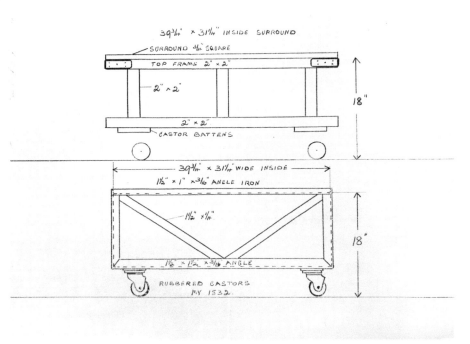

image-ideas from the past are transported into the future. But for Warburg, domesticity was also a movable feast. Perhaps the most moving architectural image in the Warburg Institute Archive was snapped on a street in Pasadena during 1895, probably by Warburg himself. In it a rather new clapboard villa is positioned for a slow flight toward the camera along an unmetalled road. The house appears rooted to the spot (no motive power is visible, either equestrian or motorized, which might nudge it into action). But it is equally clearly on the point of departure: great bogie wheels are mounted beneath it, prepared for its advance. Given the architectural history of the Warburg Institute, this image seems prescient, suggesting a principle of dwelling mortgaged both to stasis and translation, to a ghostly past and an imminent future. Logically enough, the final element in the triangulation that defines a Warburgian architecture is concerned with this ambivalent notion of the house.

The extraordinary history of Warburg's own library instantiated the possibility that a building might be considered in terms of *Bilder-fahrzeuge* in a very Warburgian way. At once an extension of Aby Warburg's private realm at Heilwigstrasse 114, and at the same time organized as a separate identifiable cultural institution, the Kultur-wissenschaftliche Bibliothek Warburg (KBW) can be seen as a machine for storing images, and for elucidating the kinds of connections between them that the notion of *Bilderfahrzeuge* permitted. The project attempted to transpose a set of working practices that had evolved in the domestic settings of Warburg's home, and in doing so constituted the first removal of the library in which a previous architectural manifestation was, in some sense, reinscribed.[22] The abrupt translation of the Institute to London aboard the HAPAG coasting steamer *Hermia* introduced a vehicular character into this Warburgian experience, one that coupled duration with displacement. When the Warburg scholars left Hamburg, significant portions of

7 Wolf Netter & Jacobi "Lipman" shelving. Stack room, KBW. Photographic album, 1926.

8 Spiral staircase, KBW. Photographic album, 1926.

9 Tecton, Sketch for a portable catalogue trolley. Warburg Institute Library, Thames House, 1934.

the material fabric that made up the library moved with them—stack-room shelving, catalogue drawers, tables, chairs, and some timber fittings travelled together with the books and the collection of glass plates from the photographic collection.[23] In later manifestations of the Institute these artifacts, as well as the relational systems for which they had been created, lived on in what Warburg might have called *Nachleben*: "afterlives." The connections appear to have been made through a combination of allusion and literal reuse. At Thames House, in the interior that the Warburg Institute commissioned from the architectural cooperative Tecton during 1933, mass-produced metal system-shelving, supplied for the KBW by the well-known German steel fabricator Wolf Netter & Jacobi, was copied on a be-spoke basis by an English metalworks to multiply the shelf run.[24] In the first sketch drafts for that interior, the chamfered corner-shelving that had been moved from the mezzanine of the reading room in Hamburg was included in the proposals for the reading room in London.[25] This literal formal copying was later abandoned, but the allusion remained: the Zeis epidiascope was remounted on axis in London as it had been in Hamburg, marking the centre of the reading room, mounted on a rostrum that echoed the lost curve of the Hamburg building's ellipse, and that was produced in stained oak to match the other shelving.[26] As in Hamburg, the reading room at Thames House was located on a ground floor, lit by five bays in the façade, a large amount of sky visible. In one sense, to sit here was to sit again in the atmosphere of a building lost: the slanting sun and silver-grey skies would have cast similar interior lights in both places.

In the subsequent history of the Warburg scholars' involvement with architecture, this system of literal reuse and invocational allusion continued. Industrial metal lighting introduced to illuminate the Wolf Netter & Jacobi shelving in the book stacks at Thames House migrated into the faux-Gothic environs of the Imperial Institute.[27] In the move from the Imperial Institute to the new building in Woburn Square, Gertrud Bing, as director, made a forensic analysis to establish which chattels of the Institute could be saved and transferred in the move.[28] In some cases this ensured that old friends were packed up together with the books (you can find book trolleys from Hamburg in the Warburg Institute even today). But the process resulted in reuse at a more microscopic scale: instructions were issued about re-staining the fronts of individual card catalogue drawers to make sure they matched the new settings, for example.[29] At the same time, the building at Woburn Square was generated through allusion. Planning the building, Saxl dreamt of resurrecting the spiral stair that had connected the reading room in Hamburg with the stack-rooms above it.[30] The siting of the reading room in juxtaposition with the bustling city outside, familiar from Thames House, was repeated, allowing scholars a constant view of taxis and pedestrians moving along Torrington Place. The building's sectional organization

10

echoed the four-storeyed book bunker suspended above the ground floor of the library in Hamburg. "Mnemosyne" was reinscribed over the door.[31] This habit offered another form of architectural nesting. Where the Planetarium embedded architectural projects and models of them within each other in space, the buildings that the Warburg Institute and its directors occupied after the move from Hamburg tended to nest architectural projects in time. To dwell in these houses was to dwell at once in a new organization and within an architectural echo of something removed.

One might point to two final examples of the significance of ghostly models that seem to be part of Warburg architecture, which refer to its two principal forms of nesting. On one side, and relating to the history of the library proper, there is the story of the physical

10 Fritz Saxl and
Gertrud Bing, late 1930s.

manifestation of the catalogue. The catalogue provided a model of the library; the cabinets spatialized that order, holding index cards that carried information about the provenance and location of each volume. In a repeated history, the arrangement of these cabinets became part of the architectural story of the Warburg Institute. In Hamburg, stained-oak drawers were built into the panelling of the reading room and lined a little chamber on its mezzanine. Wheeled catalogue trolleys were proposed at Thames House, making the whole catalogue mobile, as the space of the book stacks was opened up to readers. They were never built but the architect provided detailed drawings and obtained quotes for their construction.[32] The nature of the physical catalogue was repeatedly discussed during the development of the Institute's new home in Woburn Square and the design proposed was changed three times.[33] Standing isolated before north-facing windows, the catalogue case eventually manifested itself as a double-aspect, shoulder-high, modular slab-on-legs, with something of the proportions of Le Corbusier's exactly contemporary Unité d'habitation. This object accommodated within its standardized drawers all the variation that filled the library, providing a mirror of the holdings ordered by author on one side and subject on the other. But because the spatial disposition of the library was thought out in parallel with the architectural design, the catalogue cabinet modelled also that architectural idea: like the dumb black boxes standing in the Planetarium, it instantiated an order that informed the building it occupied.

The other example speaks to the strange quality that unified the permanent and the conditional in many of the projects connected to the itinerant Warburg Institute. In 1934, Fritz Saxl and Gertrud Bing commissioned, from the architect who had designed the interiors for the newly relocated library in Thames House, a cottage for themselves.[34] It was to be situated just outside the rapidly expanding city, at Elstree Hill in Bromley. One of the strangest idiosyncrasies of this design was its insistence that the two clients, who were proposing to live together, should have two separate entrances into the house. These were present in two sketch designs, one labelled "Saxl" and the other "Bing," on the architect's final plan. When the pair later moved into the home they shared until Saxl's death, and which Bing thereafter continued to occupy, this odd arrangement was inscribed as a physical rather than an aspirational device: visitors were to choose between a front door for Saxl facing the street and another for Bing around the side. Rather nondescript ("a high, ugly, narrow, commonplace affair in its anonymous street"), the house was situated, like the unrealized cottage, in leafy south London, this time in Dulwich.[35] To contemporaries it conveyed a curious simultaneity that communicated an ephemeral and an absolutely enduring quality: "here and now, place and time, being here, past precipitated in present."[36] If the planetarium exhibition, the library in Hamburg,

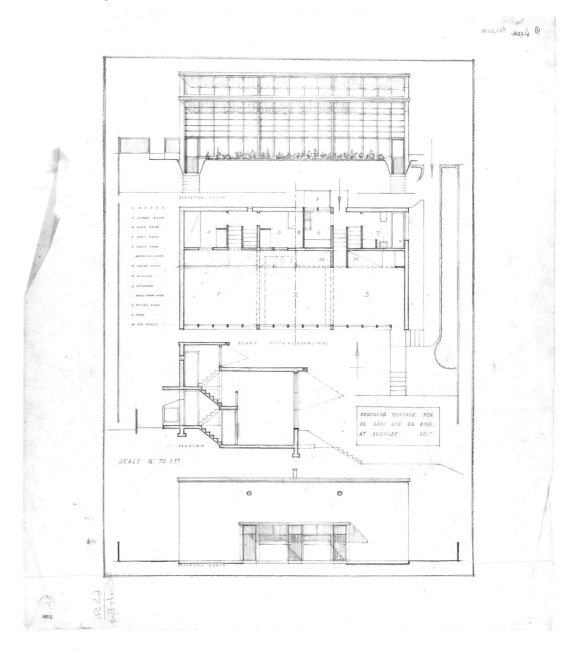

and the various reinscriptions of the Warburg Institute might be seen as *Bilderfahrzeuge*—vehicular constructions that choreographed texts and images in space, and carried them through time—Saxl and Bing's cottage suggests that this way of conceptualizing architecture in terms of reinscription might expand beyond the boundaries of an institution specifically dedicated to the research of the past. The ghosts and echoes that surround the architectures of the Warburg Institute are as much those of immediate and adjacent domestic lives as they are of distant influences or removed historical events.

11 Godfrey Samuel, Early project for a cottage for Fritz Saxl and Gertrud Bing, 1934.

BUILDING BIOGRAPHIES

Kulturwissenschaftliche Bibliothek Warburg, 1926–33

116 Heilwigstrasse, Hamburg, adjacent to Aby Warburg's home
Commissioned by the Warburg family, 1923–26
Design by Gerhard Langmaack with contributions from Fritz Schumacher, chief building director, Hamburg

1926–33 Kulturwissenschaftliche Bibliothek Warburg (KBW)
1933–93 Miscellaneous commercial functions (Neue Deutsche Wochenschau Gesellschaft mbH, Pharmachemie, etc.)
1983 Listed monument
1993 Purchased by the City of Hamburg
1993– Warburg-Haus, run by Aby-Warburg-Stiftung

Sectional Model, Kulturwissenschaftliche Bibliothek Warburg, 1926, 1:75
Model makers: Nora Kilstad and Cathrine Tønseth Sundem (2021)
MDF, cardboard, 3D-printed nylon, foam, wood filler, paper, glue, spray paint
NCS 4050-R10B derived from the spine colour code for letter M ("17th & 18th C., 18th & 19th C. 1 / England") in the 1934 Warburg catalogue system

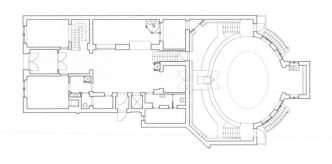

Plan ground floor, KBW, Hamburg, 1926
Redrawn 2023

In 1923, with Aby Warburg ill, Fritz Saxl was asked to supervise initial designs for a new building that would move the activities of Warburg's library out of the confines of his home at 114 Heilwigstrasse onto a gap-site next door in the recently built terrace, purchased by the Warburg family for this purpose. Early in 1924 Saxl contacted a local architect, Felix Ascher, who drew up plans. While this project was necessary because of the library's expansion, Ascher's drawings suggest that there was also a desire to reinscribe aspects of the library "as found." The project followed the sectional disposition of the big, suburban villa attached to it, and scholars were to work in its stackrooms, whose scale duplicated the domestic spaces in the private house next door.[1] Following Warburg's return to Hamburg in August, the project went through several iterations, involving the city's well-connected *Baudirektor*, Fritz Schumacher, and a young architect, Gerhard Langmaack. In that development, book stacks were quarantined off from visiting readers and placed over four floors in the reinforced concrete bunker at the centre of the building. Research was to be undertaken and discussed in a *Lese- und Vortragssaal* (reading and lecture room), projecting as a single-storey elliptical space into the garden.

At the KBW, the library that hovered, half hidden, above the ceremonial ground storey was organized to resonate with the order of its container. The work of fitting the library to the architecture was highly collaborative—it involved a whole group of Warburg's *Mitarbeiter*—and it was iterative. Attention focused first on the form and organization of the library as the armature around the library in Hamburg took shape, much inspired by its ambition to orchestrate a system of serendipity in the creation of new insight on the extremely broad range of historical material Warburg had collected. This principle, which Warburg called "the law of the good neighbour," required not that the location of books be fixed within an abstract bibliographical system, but that they should be placed organically—and indeed tentatively—in small groupings organized by associative relationships among the titles collected in each. By 1926, Warburg was

1 Stackroom, KBW,
late 1920s.

2 Entrance, KBW.
Photographic album, 1926.

annotating the floor levels of the final architectural section: *Kunst*, *Astrologie-Religion-Philosophie*, *Sprache-Geschichte*, *Krieg-Neuere Geschichte*.[2] By 1927, the final thematic series of *Bild*, *Orientierung*, *Wort*, and *Handlung* had been defined. Although the contents of the individual sections continued to be debated, the system was used to organize the four levels of book stacks, the books themselves, and the photographic collection. One might say that the crystalline intellectual structure of the library—its *idea*—emerged through matching a defined architectural organization with a thematic and tentative order of problems. Gertrud Bing, who had the job of thinking through the nitty-gritty of what this process actually meant, left an acute sense of this evolution.[3] She made small notes that listed the subject sections of the library across its various divisions. Positioned over the building's plans, these reveal themselves as tracings—notations with which possible arrangements of intellectual order could rapidly be tested against the architecture.

Architectural and intellectual systems of organization were tightly matched at the KBW, and the relationship between architecture and bibliographic order was also modulated through various pieces of technology. The reading and lecture room boasted a Zeiss epidiascope projector, which threw images onto a screen pulled up out of the floor. Book searches used a *Rohrpostapparat*, or vacuum postal system, to move requests from the reading room to the librarians above. A complicated system of book lifts, conveyor belts, and a lifting table delivered the desired volumes back to the reader on the

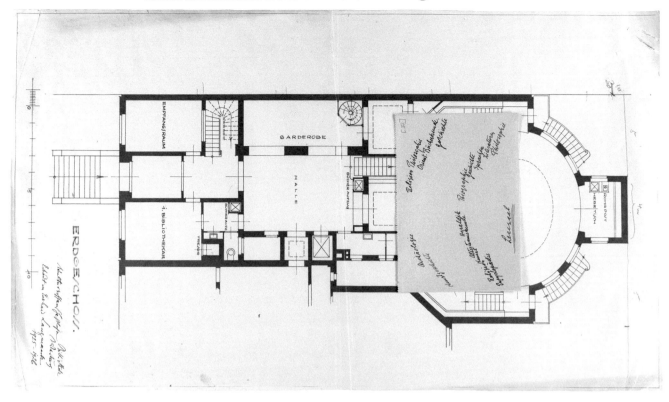

3 Hallway, KBW. Photographic album, 1926.

4 Gerhard Langmaack, Ground-floor plan, KBW, 1925–26. Overlay by Gertrud Bing showing catalogue subject headings in the reading/lecture room.

ground floor. On completing the building, Gerhard Langmaack, the architect, was commissioned to produce a photographic album recording the experience of its interiors.[4] Both the use and the style of the building were articulated distinctly in terms of its division into public areas, sumptuously lined like the interiors of an ocean liner, and private ones, with a much more sparse, machine-like character. Front of house, a view of the entrance hallway shows a book lift and its associated telephone; the epidiascope dominates the reading room. Behind the scenes, an iron spiral staircase ascends from reading room to book stacks; the low-ceilinged stackrooms are presented first bare—emphasizing the grid of Wolf Netter & Jacobi "Lipman" steel shelving they contained—and later occupied, esoteric volumes flanking narrow aisles.[5]

The stackrooms, which lay at least putatively outside the Institute's public function and were accessible only to the staff, had a magical attraction for Gertrud Bing. "The pleasure and charm of handling the books, opening them and 'browsing' as you pass along the aisles can never be replaced by a card index," she wrote in an entry in the library's *Tagebuch*, April 29, 1927—attributing the term "browsing" to an American researcher.[6] While research officially took place in the reading room, where requests had to be made for individual volumes, and linkages were already predetermined by the subject catalogue, the wilder regions of the book stacks produced something extra. The Warburg Institute commissioned blinds to be drawn down over the windows of the stackrooms, as they discovered that constant exposure to natural light faded the coloured paper strips, pasted onto the spines of the books, that articulated the associative search system on which the use of the library depended.

Hamburg Planetarium, 1930–33

Linnering 1, Stadtpark, Hamburg
Water tower commissioned by Senate of Hamburg, 1912–15
Design by Oskar Menzel
Conversion to Planetarium, 1927–30. Design by architect Hans Loop
Exhibition *Bildersammlung zur Geschichte von Sternglaube und Sternkunde* developed
by Aby Warburg and Fritz Saxl, 1927–29, completed 1930

1915–24 Water tower
1930– Hamburg Planetarium
2000–2003 Renovation, BRT Architekten
2015–17 Renovation, Limbrock Tubbesing / HJW + Partner
2021– Renovation project for reuse of upper sections of water tower by PFP Architekten

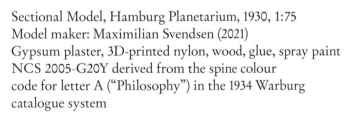

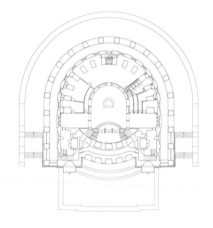

Sectional Model, Hamburg Planetarium, 1930, 1:75
Model maker: Maximilian Svendsen (2021)
Gypsum plaster, 3D-printed nylon, wood, glue, spray paint
NCS 2005-G20Y derived from the spine colour
code for letter A ("Philosophy") in the 1934 Warburg
catalogue system

Plan ground floor, Hamburg Planetarium, 1930
Redrawn 2023

Built between 1913 and 1915 to the designs of the Munich architect Oskar Menzel, the Wasserturm Winterhude was a monumental expressionist brick building in Hamburg's Stadtpark, designed by the city's *Baudirektor* Fritz Schumacher with Fritz Sperber and newly opened in 1914. Nine years after its completion, the water tower became redundant. On April 15, 1930, the Hamburg Planetarium, a city-funded project for the education of Hamburg's citizens, opened within its structure. The Hamburg architect Hans Loop provided plans that created a new modernist complex within the monumental brick structure, perforating its sides and creating a large domed auditorium in the twenty-three-metre-high cylindrical void beneath the original water tank.[1]

Warburg's possibility to exert influence over the planetarium is likely to have come via the family bank. The City of Hamburg borrowed extensively using international systems of credit to rebuild its infrastructure during the mid-1920s, loans that paid for a complete redesign of its water supply system, among other things.[2] A primary coordinator for the bond trading that realized this capital in Hamburg was M. M. Warburg & Co., with its extensive family connections in London and New York (those in New York coordinated by the American and Continental Securities Corporation, set up by Paul Warburg and others specifically for the purpose of providing loans to European actors).

A new typology, "Planetaria," which Warburg knew from examples constructed at the Zeiss factory in Jena in 1925, at the *Gesolei* exhibition in Düsseldorf in 1926, and from contemporary projects in Berlin, Munich, and Rome, made rational projections of the solar system. But because they relied on representation rather than straightforward telescopy (these were not observatories), they were places in which the history of how humanity had understood the cosmos could be staged. They were also, as Warburg was acutely aware, buildings in which the tensions between scientific truth and contemporary ideology were being played out: Warburg observed the political use made by Benito Mussolini of the opening of the Rome Planetarium while he was resident in the city in 1928.

1 Water tower in the Hamburg Stadtpark. Postcard by Knackstedt & Co., 1930.

Warburg became engaged with the proposals for a planetarium in Hamburg during 1927. By 1928 the strange possibility of creating a high-tech interior within the redundant water tower had been raised, perhaps inspired by the equally dramatic siting of the Rome Planetarium beneath the empty shell of one of the remaining vaults of the Baths of Diocletian. Something about this unexpected oddity entranced Warburg. Converted, the building would possess "an entirely unknown, and hitherto forcibly eclipsed, luminosity."[3] His attention in the project orbited around foci that appear both disparate and connected. On one side, he argued about the accessibility of the site. Warburg was absolutely convinced that a new road allowing automobiles to drive right up to the doors of the Wasserturm-turned-Planetarium would be necessary for its success, a demand that was doggedly repeated and consistently ignored.[4] On the other, he made repeated interventions concerning the kinds of objects that might be made available for the exhibition spaces. He was emphatic that his role was to loan insight rather than artifacts of material worth, offering curatorial energy rather than patronage.[5] The discussions concerned both the sources that permitted intellectual insight and the absolute centrality of technology in facilitating the means to make such an analysis speak.

The show, entitled *Bildersammlung zur Geschichte von Sternglaube und Sternkunde* (*An Image History of Astrology and Astronomy*) opened in April 1930, shortly after Warburg died, but the design principles, organization, and main exhibits were under discussion between Warburg and Saxl from 1927, and the theme was explored in two previous proposals, including one for the Museum of Technology in Munich. The "Austellung prof. Warburg," noted on the 1928 plans by Hans Loop, occupied a room that provided a tall series of apses on the external concave boundary, each lit by a high window, and two expanses of convex wall along the inner boundary.

The message of the exhibition was complex. At one level, it was a celebration of progress in human thought, an enlightenment narrative that started with the primitive figures of wandering people and concluded with the elegant calculations of Kepler. At another level, it suggested that previous structures of thought remained forever embedded in the present. Fitted into the preexisting structure of the water tower, the exhibition cycle delivered the visitor examining the last panel into the position they were in when they approached the first. At a final level, it suggested that this duration was no tyranny; that the very structures that betrayed the constant presence of the past could also create new paths and new choices for the future. The water tower as reconstructed introduced mezzanines, spatial configurations that were unforeseen by its original builders. The introductory text to the exhibition was positioned over a staircase that hugged the curving inner wall, breaking the planetary orbit implied for visitors to the main exhibition, and disappearing into a mezzanine space above the main room. Here Warburg made available key elements from his book and manuscript collection, focused on the history and development of astrology and astronomy, and coordinated the loan of further material from other Hamburg institutions.

In terms of the Warburgian themes of displacement and survival, the later history of the exhibition formed a hidden parallel with that of the Institute as a whole, in this case played out within the brick and iron structure of the water tower and in the close environs of Hamburg. Despite its provenance, the *Bildersammlung zur Geschichte von Sternglaube und Sternkunde* survived the Third Reich almost intact. In 1941 it disappeared into storage because of the war, and in 1945 the same collection of panels, objects, and maps was reopened on another site. The whole exhibition was reassembled in 1966 to mark the centenary of Warburg's birth, and two years later it was relocated to the water tower in its original form, reconstructed by Arthur Beer, a historian of astronomy who had been recruited by Warburg and Saxl to work on the original exhibition in 1928. After this the exhibition was successively corrupted: new elements were added, parts were replaced, and more modern references were introduced, until little of the original remained. In 1987, against all odds, almost the entire contents of the now lost original 1930 exhibition were rediscovered by chance in the vast disused volume of the water tower that lay above the Planetarium dome. The exhibition was saved, reexhibited in a temporary venue, and is now stored at the University of Hamburg, awaiting a promised second—or third—resurrection within the space of Oskar Menzel's much altered Wasserturm.[6]

2 *Bildersammlung zur Geschichte von Sternglaube und Sternkunde (An Image History of Astrology and Astronomy)*, exhibition, Hamburg Planetarium, 1930.

SS Hermia, 1933

Steam cargo ship (998 tonnes, l. 68.98 m, b. 10.15 m, 2 cylinders, 1 propeller, 10 knots)
Built by Flensburger Schiffsbau-Gesellschaft
Launched Flensburg, February 4, 1910, and delivered to Adolph Kirsten & Co., Hamburg

1910–28 Hamburg–London Line (Adolph Kirsten & Co.)
1928–34 Hamburg–London Line (Amerikanische Aktien Paketfahrt Gesellschaft HAPAG)
1933 December 12, transports Warburg Library holdings, furniture, and records to London (two trips)
1934 Repurchased for Hamburg–London Line (Adolph Kirsten & Co.)
1940 German Navy hospital ship. December 20, renamed *Adriana*. December 29, runs into British air mine on the Elbe near Freiburg

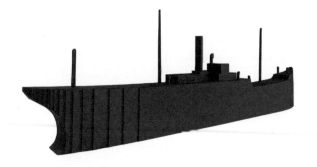

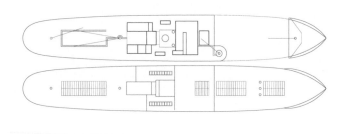

Sectional Model, SS *Hermia*, 1933, 1:75
Model maker: Mara Trübenbach (2021)
Gypsum plaster, 3D-printed nylon, wood, glue, spray paint
NCS 6502-R and 0560-Y80R derived from the
spine colour codes for letters H ("Political History")
and I ("Middle Ages I") in the 1934 Warburg
catalogue system

Plan, SS *Hermia*, 1933
Redrawn 2023

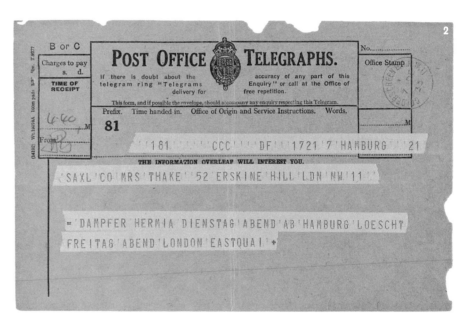

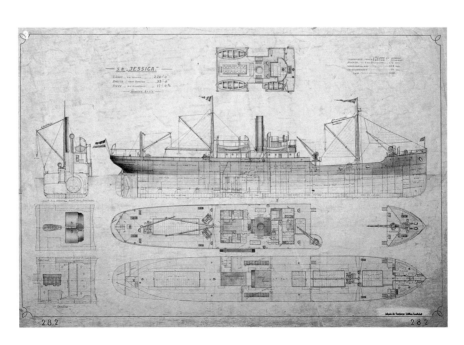

1 SS *Hermia* on the Elbe, ca. 1930.

2 Telegram from Gertrud Bing to Fritz Saxl, December 7, 1933.

3 Plan and profile drawing, SS *Jessica* (sister ship to *Hermia*), Flensburger Schiffsbau-Gesellschaft, 1908.

Thames House, 1934–37

Millbank, Westminster, London
Office building commissioned by Imperial Chemical Industries (ICI) chairman
Alfred Mond, 1927–30. Design by architect Sir Frank Baines
Interior project commissioned by the Warburg Institute 1933–34 with Fritz Saxl
as director and Gertrud Bing as assistant director
Design by architect Godfrey Samuel, Tecton

1930–65 Imperial Chemical Industries
1934–37 Warburg Institute (ground floor, south block)
1934–39 British Intelligence Service MI5 (top of south block)
1945–89 British Government offices, latterly Department of Energy
1994–2013 Northern Ireland Office
Since 1994 Primary function as MI5 Headquarters

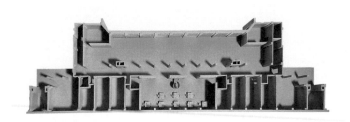

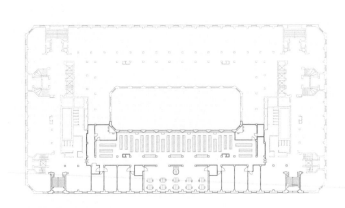

Plan Model, Warburg Institute Interiors, Thames House,
1934, 1:75
Model maker: Pål Luis Sanchez-Paredes (2021)
First floor at Thames House with entrances facing
Thorney Street
MDF, paper, glue, spray paint
NCS 1030-R10B derived from the colour for
letter G ("Oriental Antiquity") in the 1934 Warburg
catalogue system

Plan ground floor, Warburg Library, Thames House, 1934
Redrawn 2023

Their first building project in London brought the Warburg scholars into direct contact with a more international design context. The architect appointed to design the interior that was to house the library was Godfrey Samuel of the avant-garde practice Tecton, created in 1931 by a group of Architectural Association graduates together with the Russian émigré architect Berthold Lubetkin. Several Tectonites, including Samuel, were members of the Modern Architecture Research Group (MARS), founded to represent British engagement at the *Congrès Internationaux d'Architecture Moderne* in 1933. In their first years, Tecton made a speciality in designing accommodation for exotic arrivals in London.[1] At the same time as they were rehousing the Warburg Institute, they were working on the iconic Penguin Pool and Gorilla House at London Zoo. While the Gorilla House displayed a semicircular geometry as strict as that found in Saxl and Warburg's exhibition for the Hamburg Planetarium, the Penguin Pool combined an ellipse and mezzanine balconies to create an effect as theatrical as that of the *Lese- und Vortragssaal* the KBW.

The library was to be re-established on the ground floor of Thames House in Westminster, a state-of-the-art office building controlled by another set of Warburg connections, the Mond family.[2] The plan that Samuel developed for the library, a composition as

1 Reading/lecture room, Warburg Library, Thames House, ca. 1934–35.

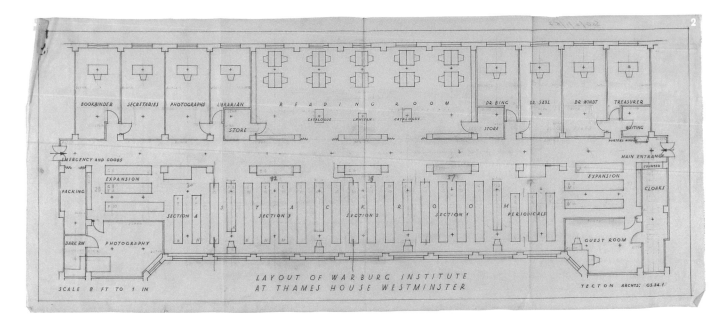

tight and symmetrical as anything else produced by Tecton during the period, oriented the proposed accommodation around a flexible-use space at the centre, that served both as a lecture and a reading room.[3]

The first London manifestation of the Warburg Library was in many senses an aspirational reinscription of a lost space. The tables and chairs that readers occupied, and the built-in bookshelves that surrounded them, were all transported from Hamburg. In May 1934, the epidiascope projector was reinstalled, exactly on axis, as it had been in Hamburg. To support it, the Warburg Library commissioned Samuel to design a bespoke rostrum in oak, stained to match the transported shelving, and curved like the back wall of the original reading room.[4]

The steel Wolf Netter & Jacobi "Lipman" shelving that had accommodated the main part of the library, and which had been so carefully photographed in Hamburg, was also reinstalled. Encountered on a single level, these stacks were now divided into four sections in a single space, with a slight variation from the order adopted in Hamburg: "Religion, Natural Science and Philosophy"; "Language and Literature"; "Fine Arts"; and "Social and Political Life."[5] An English metalworks, G. A. Harvey & Co., were commissioned to produce copies of the Lipman system to extend the shelf run. Bing was asked to supply the fabricators with samples of the original stacks so that the colour could be matched exactly.

Even as it reinscribed lost interiors, the experience of Thames House created new sets of impressions. Where the interior of the library in Hamburg had emphasized the separation of the reading room from its external context, where the librarian's niche had blocked the view and the windowsills were so high that a sitting scholar

could not see over them, in London the relationship between interior and exterior was brought up close. The reading room looked directly out over a London side street, opposite Stephen Courtauld's London Ice Club—a society magnet established in 1927—on one side, and the building site for a new office development on the other. Under the aegis of Bing and Saxl, readers in London could roam the whole collection. Linked to the reading room by wide, curtained openings, the books were laid out in full view. The timber-panelled "front-of-house" and the hard, industrial "back-of-house," separated in Hamburg, were now set in a direct visual juxtaposition. This confrontation was recorded in photography and appeared as the first image in the account that Gertrud Bing published in the *Library Association Record* in 1934.

2 Tecton, Plan, Warburg Library, Thames House, 1934.

3 Construction photograph of Thames House, Millbank, London, ca. 1930.

Cottage at Bromley, 1934–35 (unbuilt)

Elstree Hill, Bromley
House commissioned by Fritz Saxl, director, and Gertrud Bing, assistant director, Warburg Institute, 1934–35
Design by architect Godfrey Samuel, Tecton

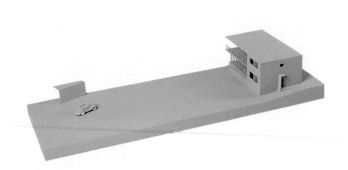

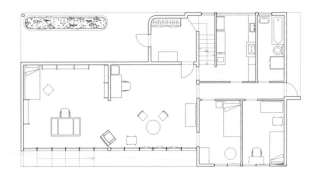

Sectional Model, Cottage at Bromley, 1:75
Model maker: Pernille Boye Ahlgren (2021)
MDF, 3D-printed nylon, wood, wood filler, paper, glue, spray paint, varnish
NCS 4020-G50Y derived from the spine colour code for letter B ("Religion; France") in the 1934 Warburg catalogue system

Plan ground floor, Cottage at Bromley, 1935
Redrawn 2023

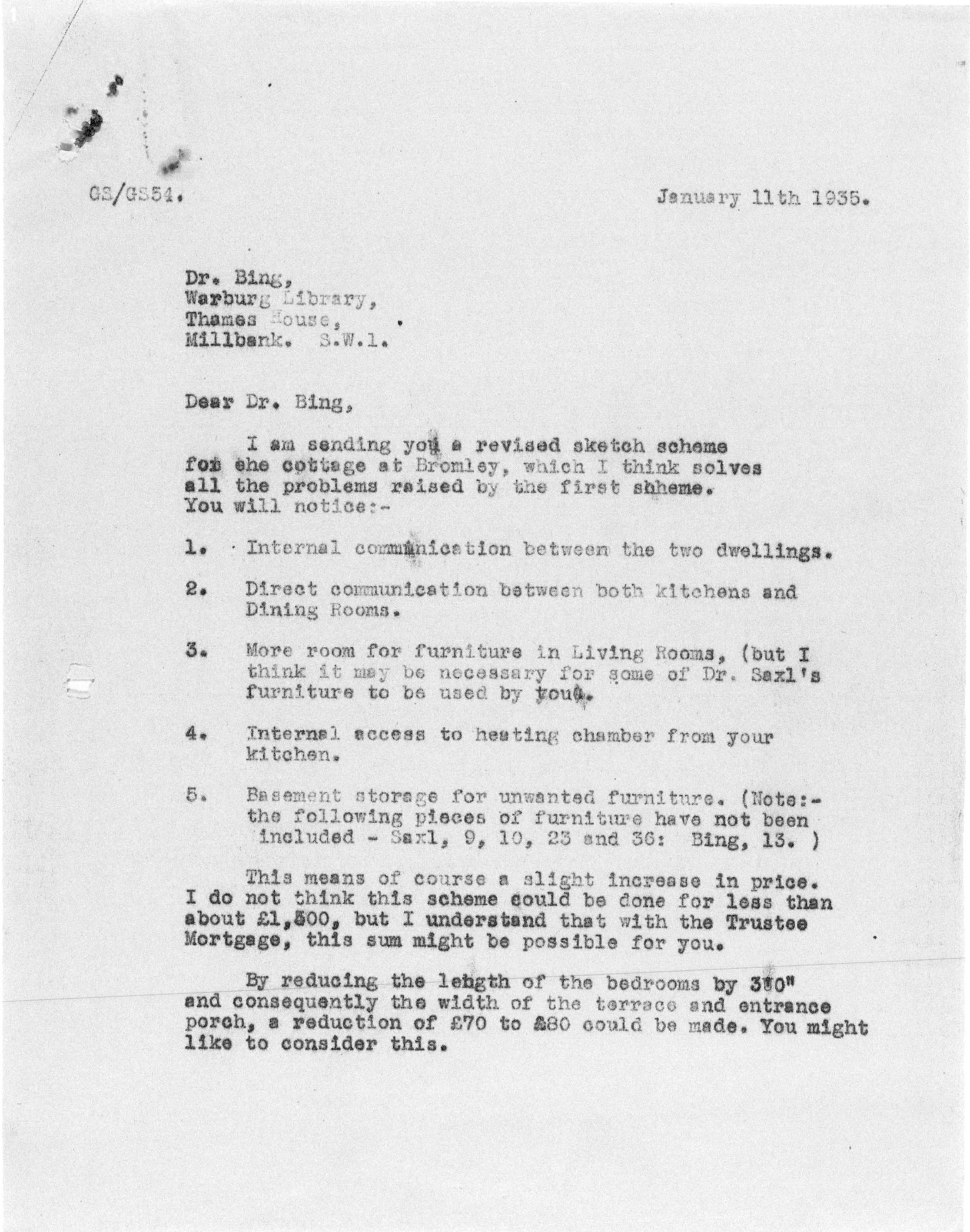

GS/GS54.   January 11th 1935.

Dr. Bing,
Warburg Library,
Thames House,
Millbank. S.W.1.

Dear Dr. Bing,

        I am sending you a revised sketch scheme
for the cottage at Bromley, which I think solves
all the problems raised by the first shheme.
You will notice:-

1.   Internal communication between the two dwellings.

2.   Direct communication between both kitchens and
        Dining Rooms.

3.   More room for furniture in Living Rooms, (but I
        think it may be necessary for some of Dr. Saxl's
        furniture to be used by you.

4.   Internal access to heating chamber from your
        kitchen.

5.   Basement storage for unwanted furniture. (Note:-
        the following pieces of furniture have not been
        included - Saxl, 9, 10, 23 and 36: Bing, 13.)

        This means of course a slight increase in price.
I do not think this scheme could be done for less than
about £1,500, but I understand that with the Trustee
Mortgage, this sum might be possible for you.

        By reducing the length of the bedrooms by 3'0"
and consequently the width of the terrace and entrance
porch, a reduction of £70 to £80 could be made. You might
like to consider this.

In 1934, as Saxl and Bing re-established the work of the Warburg
Library in the new cultural context of London, the pair enlisted the
help of their institutional architect, Godfrey Samuel, in a proposed
commission for a new house for themselves on Elstree Hill outside
London. The unbuilt project produced a number of letters and a set
of design proposals that disappeared into the archives.

        Horizontal in emphasis, the design was clearly inspired by conti-
nental models, and it resembled Samuel's later work. It is two-storeyed
with two separate—and labelled—entrances, one for Saxl and one

1 Letter from Godfrey
Samuel to Gertrud Bing,
January 11, 1930.

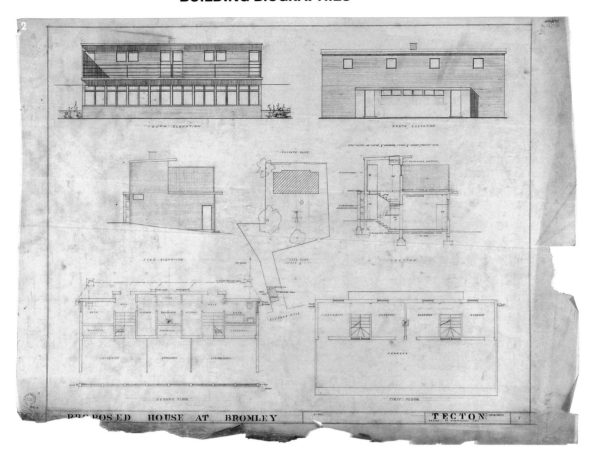

for Bing. Saxl would arrive from the west through a cut-back porch before mounting the stairs into an apartment on the first floor. Bing would enter from the east through a single door in an otherwise mute façade to her accommodation on the ground. The garden front of the house was to be largely glazed, open to sun and air. It overlooked what would clearly have become a beautiful garden with long views across open country. Some of the main functions were to be doubled as if this was two houses: two kitchens, two bathrooms, two dining rooms, and two book rooms; some were to be shared as if it was one: a furnace room (the subject of discussion in the letters and clearly very important) and a basement for storing "unwanted furniture." There is a maid's room, a guest room, and bedrooms for a daughter and a son (Saxl's childen with his estranged wife, Elise, who remained in Hamburg when Saxl moved to London to prepare for the arrival of the library). The plans make no declaration about the sleeping arrangements of the clients themselves. This reticence belies a tension. During the later 1920s Warburg and Saxl, both married, competed for Bing. Saxl appointed her in Warburg's absence. Bing acted as Warburg's muse on his return from Kreuzlingen, and the two of them went to Florence in 1927 and again to Italy for a nine-month trip in 1928–29. Wives, husbands, colleagues, and lovers existed in intimate proximity in this context. It was Bing who found Warburg dead in his study after a dinner at his home in Heilwigstrasse in Hamburg in 1929 (she had been upstairs talking to his wife). And it was Bing who conducted negotiations with Godfrey Samuel for a house with Saxl in England.

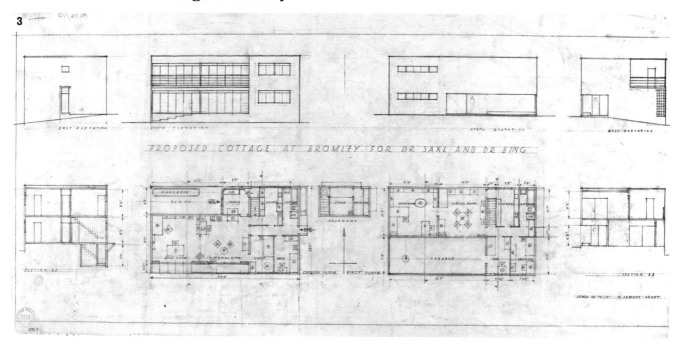

PROPOSED COTTAGE AT BROMLEY FOR DR SAXL AND DR BING

"Dear Mr. Samuel," she wrote on December 19, 1934: "We are simply delighted with the new design. It is absolutely what we should like to have. Even our furniture will go into the house, and there will be space besides to store things." This preoccupation with furniture, with the familiar chattels that moved and provided a foundation for the pattern of a life transposed, returns throughout the project correspondence. Based on an inventory supplied by Bing, Samuel noted on his plan drawing from January 1935 the whereabouts of each piece of furniture Bing and Saxl possessed. The pieces were marked by a numerical key (Saxl's furniture on loan to Bing identified by the prefix "S"), and examples of exchange between the two furniture collections were detailed in writing.[1]

Bing and Saxl lived later in a house in Dulwich, also in south London, in which they inscribed several of the patterns projected in the design for their cottage: they had two separate entrances, semi-separated accommodation and a very English, and very loved, garden. Posthumous descriptions of the pair by their friends record an intimate connection between personal identity, furniture, and establishment also in this setting. For Donald Gordon, Bing seemed "always to have been behind a table ... that desk in the tiny room at the Imperial Institute ... the huge black post-Bauhaus desk in her room in Dulwich."[2] In Michael Baxandall's recollection of the same house, "Bing sat at the desk [in Saxl's study]—oneself in a very German chair."[3] The building projected at once a sense of the absolutely temporary and an aura of long-term occupation. "Bing spoke of Saxl's elusiveness, his acceptance of the provisional, his wish to be free.... Yet, and always yet, there was that garden designed and planted and cherished ... a maturity that would take years to come."[4]

2 Godfrey Samuel, Early project for a cottage for Fritz Saxl and Gertrud Bing, 1934.

3 Godfrey Samuel, Final project for a cottage for Fritz Saxl and Gertrud Bing, 1934–35.

Imperial Institute Buildings, 1937–59

South Kensington, London
Building project initiated by HRH Edward, Prince of Wales, after the Golden
Jubilee of Her Majesty Queen Victoria, 1886-93
Design by architect Thomas Edward Collcutt. Inaugurated by Queen Victoria,
May 10, 1893. Demolished 1957-65
Interior conversions commissioned by the Warburg Institute 1937 and 1952 with
Fritz Saxl and Henri Frankfort as directors and Gertrud Bing as assistant director
Design by W. Cox & Partners and others

1887 Foundation stone laid
1893–1958 Imperial Institute
1935–57 Warburg Institute (east wing)
1958–62 Commonwealth Institute
1962 Main structure demolished to make way for the building of Imperial College

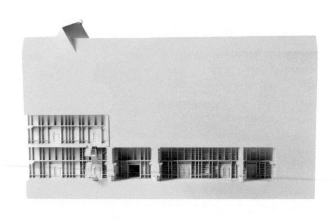

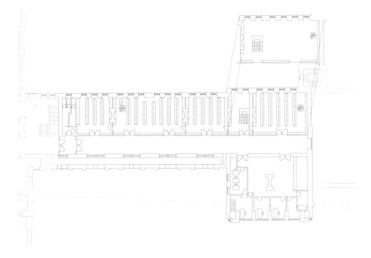

Sectional Model, Warburg Library, Imperial Institute
Building, 1934, 1:75
Model makers: Pernille Boye Ahlgren, Christian
Tømmeraas Berg, Anne Lise Ladegård (2021-23)
MDF, hard foam, 3D-printed plaster and nylon,
wood, wood filler, glue, spray paint, varnish
NCS 0510-B30G derived from the spine colour
code for letter O ("Switzerland") in the 1934 Warburg
catalogue system

Plan ground and first floor, Warburg Institute,
Imperial Institute Buildings east wing, 1952
Redrawn 2023

After two years at Thames House, by 1936 discussions were in train that led to the removal of the library to the Imperial Institute Buildings in South Kensington, where the Warburg Institute stayed until 1958. In terms of fulfilling the architectural potential within Warburg's system of thought, the occupation of these interiors was crucial. The rooms at the Imperial Institute formed the context for Frances Yates's investigations into the relations between architecture, memory, and the organization of knowledge, published in *Giordano Bruno and the Hermetic Tradition* (1961) and *The Art of Memory* (1965), and formed the architectural framework of the thinking contained in her *Theatre of the World* (1969). In the same rooms, Rudolf Wittkower met with a young Colin Rowe to discuss the symbolic significance of architectural arrangement and proportion, evolving ideas later to be published in Rowe's "The Mathematics of the Ideal Villa," which appeared in *Architectural Review* in 1947, and in Wittkower's *Architectural Principles in the Age of Humanism* (1949). And it was from offices in the Imperial Institute Buildings that Fritz Saxl, Henri Frankfort, and Gertrud Bing, as successive directors of the Warburg Institute, worked with the University of London on plans for a new building after 1944.

The encounter with the Imperial Institute put the Warburg Library into juxtaposition with a third, phantasmagorical, architecture. Where Thames House had offered the open-plan floor plate of a modern office building, the Imperial Institute offered a suite of heavily moulded, double-height rooms within a stylistically eclectic building dominated by monstrous flying stone staircases and endless, monumental corridors. At first, at least, the entire contents of the library could be swallowed by the peripheral shelving these rooms provided, meaning that its other functions could be located in and

1 Reading room, Warburg Institute, Imperial Institute Buildings, ca. 1952.

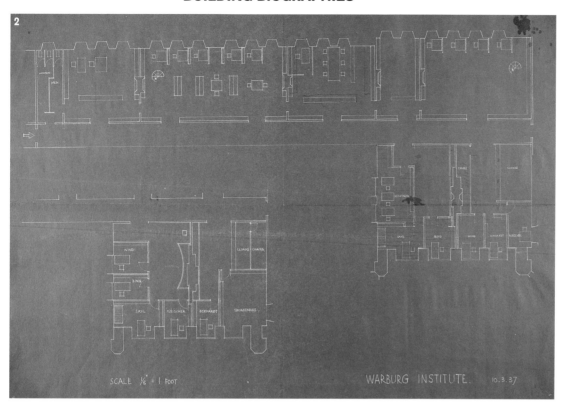

among the books, an arrangement very close to that which Felix Ascher had envisaged for Fritz Saxl in 1924. Gertrud Bing, describing the arrangement at the Imperial Institute in 1937, was emphatic that the problem of image was central to the library's activities. This section, now titled "Art and Archaeology," surrounded scholars working in the main reading room, which occupied the second, and largest, space in the enfilade sequence. "Language and Literature" occupied the walls around the third and fourth rooms, whose centres were occupied by the photographic collection, overseen by Rudolf Wittkower, and by Anthony Blunt and his editing activities respectively.[1] The final double-height room in the sequence was given over to "Religion, Natural Science and Philosophy," and the mezzanine of the very first to the "History of Social Forms." The order of sections adopted at Thames House had been reversed.[2]

The superimposition of functions that this initial arrangement created was to be short-lived. As the library grew, the central areas of the various rooms began to be given over to freestanding book stacks and in 1951 the Warburg took over the suite of enfilade rooms directly above those it already occupied on the ground floor.[3] The arrangement that resulted can be viewed as nightmarish or inspirational. For one young scholar in the Institute, Sydney Anglo, it created a jack-in-the-box quality of unexpectedness. A quality of imminent surprise was created by the staircase that the Institute had constructed to connect the spaces on the ground and first floor. It rose incongruously out of the room previously occupied by Anthony Blunt and arrived directly into the middle of a new reading room above, through a hole cut in the Victorian structure. As Anglo recalled: "It was an especial treat, when seated there, to hear climbing

footsteps of some approaching scholar, to try to guess who it was, and to watch a learned head rising up through the opening in the floor."[4] The organization of the space put the unfamiliar into very intimate juxtaposition with the familiar.

This same quality of violent juxtaposition is evident also in the photographic record of the building made following its expansion in 1952. The first-floor reading room seems chaotic, its central staircase clearly visible, busts of Fritz Saxl and Warburg himself staring down impassively from the mantelpiece. On the lower level the juxtaposition between the industrial and the gentlemanly, implicit at the KBW and explicit at Thames House, was compressed brutally. Metre-module metal shelving filled the rooms entirely, surrounded by gothicky timber linings and mezzanine balconies carried on faux-timber consoles. But although visually jarring, this reorganization re-established the idea that the library consisted of four interdisciplinary bunkers of books disposed across four main spaces. The major sections were now those on "The image" ("Archaeology and Art," in room two) and on "Orientation by means of myth, magic and logic" ("Religion; Science; Philosophy," rooms four and five); the smaller those on "The significant Act" ("Social and Political Life," room one) and on "The Word" ("Literature; Transmission of Classical Learning," room three).[5] In this guise the library regained some of its sense of being a recombinatory machine set up in an opulent architectural frame.

2 Cox & Partners, Proposed conversion plan drawing, Warburg Institute, Imperial Institute Buildings, March 1937.

3 Staircase, Imperial Institute Buildings. *The Builder*, 1892.

Woburn Square, 1958–

Woburn Square, Bloomsbury, London
Building commissioned 1948–58 by the University of London with
Henri Frankfort and Gertrud Bing as directors of the Warburg Institute
Design by Adams Holden & Pearson
Currently undergoing renovation as the Warburg Renaissance project
by Haworth Tompkins, London

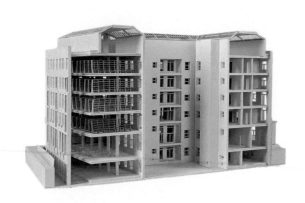

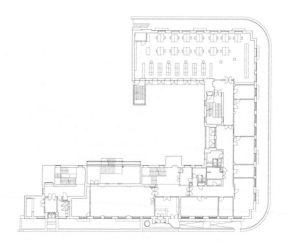

Sectional Model, Warburg Institute, Woburn Square, 1:75
Model makers: Karina Tang, Silje Ekornrud Seim,
Amalie Elvegård Utigård (2021)
MDF, veneer, paper, glue, spray paint
NCS S0515-Y40R derived from the spine colour
code for letter L ("Spain") in the 1934 Warburg
catalogue system

Plan ground floor, Warburg Institute, Woburn Square, 1958
Redrawn 2023

The proposal for a new building for the Warburg Institute was made within the master plan developed by Charles Holden for London University. Initially the Warburg was to form part of a low bi-institutional building with the Courtauld Institute of Art, with the Warburg Library housed mainly in its basement.[1] Events in the early 1950s challenged this arrangement and by 1954 a new scheme was in place that positioned the Warburg Institute alone on its current corner site, terminating the vista along Torrington Place. The library was to be spread over four floors above the reading room, as it had been in Hamburg. Gertrud Bing took over the role of client representative for the project in March 1954, and by August that year a final footprint was established and the scheme was exhibited at the Imperial Institute Buildings.[2] The detailed scheme-design was finalized by June 1955.

The appearance and organization of the "new building" was conceived of in very different terms by the various actors involved. For the University and its architect, a combined Courtauld and Warburg building was to be low, neoclassical, and, specifically, American: The Fogg Museum of Art at Harvard University, with Felix Warburg as a main donor for its 1920 building campaign, remained a "parent" institution for the combined Courtauld and Warburg Institutes in terms of its brief.[3] Drawings from Holden's office in the RIBA collection show how literally this requirement was taken by the architects.[4]

For Saxl, the new building projected memory into the future. Specifying "Needs of the Warburg Institute" in 1945, he dreamt, just as he had in Hamburg, of readers' carrels in the windows of the stackrooms. He bearded Holden on the possibility of squeezing four levels of library into the University's plan for a three-floor building.

1 Lecture room,
Warburg Institute, 1958.

And he asked that "a small winding staircase should lead from the reading room to the stackrooms."[5] Henri Frankfort, who succeeded Saxl as director, was committed to organizing its library horizontally.[6] Gertrud Bing sought a very different architectural mindset from that exhibited by the elderly Holden and the Building Committee. In March 1953 she wrote to a contact in Rome asking for advice on alternative designers.[7]

Whatever these disparate ideas about form and appearance, in the end the arrangement chosen had resonances with several of its former homes. There was something of the Hamburg library in the classicizing fenestration and modular bays of the lecture room proposed at Woburn Square, with its quiet view of leafy gardens and a distant terrace beyond. And the arrangement that Bing approved in 1954, which situated the reading room like a lighthouse, facing London's bustle up Torrington Place, repeated the dramatic juxtaposition created at Thames House, where readers looked directly into the street.

Just as revealing about the way in which the Warburg scholars furnished their new home with memories of the old are the resonances between the stackrooms at Woburn Place and those of its Hamburg ancestor. While the area of the building in London was much larger, the stackrooms were again arranged in four floors over the reading room; in both places books were stored in rooms low in height, filled with stove enamel metal shelving and lit by fluorescent tubes that ran above the aisles between them. Drop-cords were positioned in a special arrangement directly over the ends of each book stack, the cord threaded through a metal bracket that carried signage

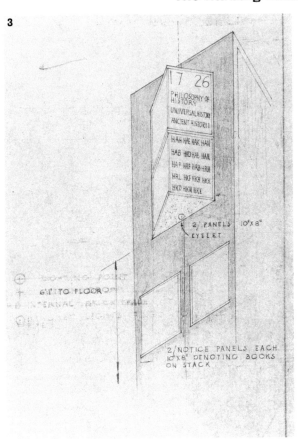

identifying the class marks to be found in each section. Retrieving a book at the Warburg was a distinctive, gestural experience. One entered the stackroom; one located the subheading at a distance and the class mark close-to at the end of the stacks; one raised a hand to pull the drop-cord; one extracted the book.

Architectural projects always involve painstaking attention to detail, but few clients enter into that detail as Bing appears to have done. The final result of her care was a new library that seems, immediately, to have had a lived-in quality, one in which new rituals of use rapidly took on a habitual feel. Architectural critics and certain academics panned the new building ("like a 1930s telephone exchange" according to Nikolaus Pevsner; "bleak and unthinking" according to Michael Baxandall). But, as she unpacked in 1958, Bing took a notably more optimistic tone:

"Even I am beginning to think that we shall be quite happy once routine comes into its own again and the Institute is being used in the normal way. The library is certainly very well provided for, spacious, well-lit, and in a short time it will be also well sign-posted."[8]

The rotational journey of searching—from reading room catalogue to stackroom signage, and from stackroom signage to light switch, to shelf and back to reading room—made for a powerful, haptic experiential pattern. As much as anything, perhaps, this re-inscription of the everyday through furniture and ritual sustained the Warburg Institute's enduring investigation into the cultural significance of survival.

2 First-floor stacks, Warburg Institute, Woburn Square, 1958.

3 Adams Holden & Pearson Architects, Setting-out diagram of lighting points and drop switches in Warburg Institute, September 1956. Detail.

TRIANGULATIONS

The Elliptical Reading Room as Denkraum

Claudia Wedepohl

The most iconic element of the purpose-built Kulturwissenschaftliche Bibliothek Warburg (KBW) at Heilwigstrasse 116 was its combination reading room and lecture hall. At the core of the building that would house his library, his lifetime achievement, Aby Warburg wanted to see a personally meaningful symbolic form translated into architectural form: the ellipse. Symbolic in a twofold way, the dipoles of the ellipse, for him, not only represented the latent bipolarity of the human mind, but also made allusion to the striving for a mathematically exact calculation of the orbits of the planets and thus to a crucial leap in human understanding of nature through scientific means.

During a three-year stay (1921–24) in Ludwig Binswanger's private clinic in Kreuzlingen, while Warburg was slowly recovering from his mental breakdown and regaining control over his own thoughts, he had reflected on how and when in the history of European civilization the transition from speculation to calculation in arriving at a conception of the world order had occurred.[1] In doing so, he had focused on the role of the German astronomer and mathematician Johannes Kepler (1571–1630) within the progression generally known as the "scientific revolution" or "scientific turn."[2] In 1922–23, as he reviewed his earlier ideas about cultural-historical change in the Italian Quattro- and Cinquecento—namely his studies on Borso d'Este's (1413–1471) fresco cycle of the twelve months in the Palazzo Schifanoia in Ferrara,[3] and on Bernardo Buontalenti's (1531–1608) costume designs of 1588–89 for the musical-allegorical *Intermedi* of the comedy *La Pellegrina*[4]—he had become convinced that this transition was a three-step process: firstly, the re-establishment of the ancient model of the cosmos as a harmonic system of celestial spheres; secondly, the acceptance that the cosmos does not consist only of regular forms; and thirdly, the conviction that an empirical approach to nature was required to establish fundamental facts.

The first signs of a revival of the spherical model (with the seven known planets orbiting around the earth) revealed themselves to Warburg in the planimetric depiction of the twelve months in the Palazzo Schifanoia, each divided into three horizontal registers: earth, the region of the fixed stars (i.e., the zodiac), and the region of the Olympian gods. Reserving the highest region for the Olympians demonstrated to him a new appreciation for the ethical principles these gods represented. His proof of the adoption of classical ideas was the subsequent staging of the origin of the harmony of the spheres in the first of Count Giovanni de' Bardi's (1534–1612) *Intermedi* of 1589. Produced for the wedding of Grand Duke Ferdinando I de' Medici (1549–1609) and Christine of Lorraine (1565–1637) as a display of technological capacity and power, Bardi's *Intermedi* were inspired by Plato's *Myth of Er*, and had the Sirens perform an eight-part madrigal on stage (with a Siren producing a tone for each of the celestial spheres). In 1895 Warburg had studied not only the panegyrical iconographies of Bardi's *Intermedi* but also their origin, namely the influence of the late-antique poet Martianus Capella, who, in his *De Nuptiis Philologiae et Mercurii* (fifth century), had replaced Plato's singing Sirens with the Muses. Putting Helios-Apollo, the leader of the Muses, at the universe's centre turned the cosmic model into an allegory of man's striving for knowledge, cognition, and enlightenment. For Warburg, this concept was the origin of the heliocentrism on whose acceptance he believed Nicolaus Copernicus's (1473–1543) calculations were based. Yet no one before Kepler had mastered the transition from an anthropocentric and/or anthropomorphic conception of the world, characteristic of religious attitudes, to the objectivity of modern sciences via the abstractions of philosophy. Kepler reflected on this transition explicitly; in his *De motibus stellae Martis* of 1609 he laid out how he had calculated the elliptical orbit of Mars and thus metaphorically overcame the planet's presumed negative influences on his children. The insight that this publication marked a watershed moment in the history of civilization, gained in Kreuzlingen, far away from the resources of his library, became for Warburg a symbol of his reclaimed mental capacities. When his younger colleague, the philosopher Ernst Cassirer (1874–1945), informed him during a visit in 1924 that Kepler indeed knew the ancient Greek geometer Apollonius of Perga's work on conic sections, including the ellipse—one of the fundamental forms in geometry—his hypothetical idea, that only an acceptance of the ellipse as a natural form allowed the historical breakthrough, was confirmed.[5]

Crucial for this transition from a subjective to an objective view, according to Warburg, was a healthy scepticism toward traditional truths. He saw this scepticism emerging in a newly won self-confidence, perceived as a dynamic vitality, which he found reflected in commissions by the Italian merchant-banker elite, such as Francesco Sassetti (1421–1490)

Gerhard Langmaack,
Perspective section of the
reading/lecture room,
KBW, Hamburg, ca. 1925.

and Agostino Chigi (1466-1520), and later in treatises on the laws of nature by figures including the engineer and mathematician Camillo Agrippa (before 1535-ca. 1598). To explain the underlying cognitive processes which he believed were responsible for regress and progress in the history of civilization, Warburg drew upon the imagery of both electrodynamics and mechanical physics. For his preferred metaphor, the oscillating pendulum, he merged the physics of tension force through gravitation with that of energy generation in an electromagnetic field. The resulting model, resonating throughout his oeuvre, is based on the established concepts of "polarity" (e.g., Tito Vignoli's theory of myth and science as evolutionary opposites, and Friedrich Nietzsche's theory of the Dionysian and the Apollonian as psychological opposites), but the association of human vitality with energy generation was of his own making.[6] Translated to the mind, Warburg construed a spectrum between the poles of identification and abstraction, with memory stored in matter (either the human body or its mirror, the image) defined as an inspiring energy reserve. For patrons such as Sassetti or Chigi this meant vacillating between traditional Christian beliefs and trust in themselves, encouraged by classical models which preserved the energy of mankind's experience and knowledge. Periods of crisis and transition brought a latent bipolarity to the fore. Johannes Kepler was, too, for Warburg the incarnation of a "transitional" type who mastered both astrology and astronomy; his progress was enabled by recognizing the significance of the ellipse.

Following a first design by the famous *Oberbaudirektor* Fritz Schumacher (1869-1947), Warburg's young architect, Gerhard Langmaack (1898-1986), needed thirteen further drafts and a model to reach a satisfactory practical solution for constructing a large elliptical room on an exceptionally narrow plot. In March 1925 he and Warburg settled on a plan for a squared oblong room with curving shelves for a *Handbibliothek* and journals, drawers for the catalogue cards, tables and chairs, a lectern, a retractable screen, a niche for a librarian's desk, and a gallery with collapsible chairs and projectors, all lit by a great elliptical skylight.[7]

Critics have viewed the room, for which an open-stack shelving system was sacrificed, as almost sacred. Although an oval room at the centre was not without precedent in library buildings, the shape, incorporating a symbol of the constant struggle to gain rationality and to fight the irrational through learning and knowledge, remains unique.[8] For Warburg, the ellipse was the embodiment of the epitome of abstract thought: an ideal room for reflection and thus a metaphorical *Denkraum*.

The Hamburg Planetarium as a Problem Building

Uwe Fleckner

The desire for spatial orientation is an astonishing constant in Aby Warburg's otherwise "wild" thinking. It emerges when he diagrams the spheres of influence in his own life, when he maps his travels during the 1895-96 journey to the United States, or when he sketches out drawings showing the continental drift of exchange processes in the history of art and culture, in order to create geographical overviews of the afterlife of archaic and antique image-ideas.[1] The arrangement of his own library, whose levels stratified fields of knowledge—word, image, orientation, and action—also testifies to a will to spatial orientation on the part of this art historian.

When Warburg was planning the exhibition *Bildersammlung zur Geschichte von Sternglaube und Sternkunde* (*An Image History of Astrology and Astronomy*) for the Hamburg Planetarium in the last years of his life, both the building itself—a former water tower—and its urban situation were crucial to the decision to donate to his native city a "pedagogical apparatus for the educated and the uneducated," of a kind that "European society does not yet possess."[2] Warburg called the tower in Hamburg the "Lynceus Tower," a watchtower—which he understood metaphorically, of course—from which one could cast a clear-eyed gaze down into the world.[3] And this scholar, who had wrestled with orientation all his life, provided an intellectually charged interior architecture for the exhibition that he organized together with Fritz Saxl and other members of the Kulturwissenschaftliche Bibliothek Warburg (KBW).

The water tower, which had been decommissioned in 1924, was built ten years previously in Hamburg's Stadtpark, designed by the urban planner Fritz Schumacher as a place of recreation but also of education for the citizens of the Hanseatic city between 1912 and 1914. Warburg promised the city's school board to create in the remodelled building a permanent exhibition on the history of astrology as an "offshoot to the K.B.W."[4] In the autumn of 1928 he told his friend the philosopher Ernst Cassirer:

"Probably—if the legislature so grants—I can expect from the state a fine site for my cosmologicon, i.e. for the series of images that seeks to illustrate the development of astral symbolism: the Zeiss Planetarium is to be built into the currently unused water tower and, in accordance with my doggedly pursued idea, will be accompanied by an introduction into the pre-Keplerian way of thinking through this very exhibition, which will be displayed on all the lower-floor walls. Even a reading room on the upper floor and an auditorium (which I will have to share with the Planetarium, but has, if necessary, room for 350 people and also has a Zeiss projector) will be part of it".[5]

Besides the exhibition, this auditorium and the reading room—a study library consisting of works on loan from the KBW and other Hamburg institutions—would be used to fulfil Warburg's ambitions for a groundbreaking popular education.[6]

Working from the art historian's ideas, Hans Loop, the architect who had been commissioned to convert the water tower, designed the exhibition space, a meeting room ("Konferenz-Zimmer"), and an office for Aby Warburg on the ground floor of the building. The collection of images itself was to be displayed in a room with the form of a segmental arch, divided by the existing pillars of the enormous struc-

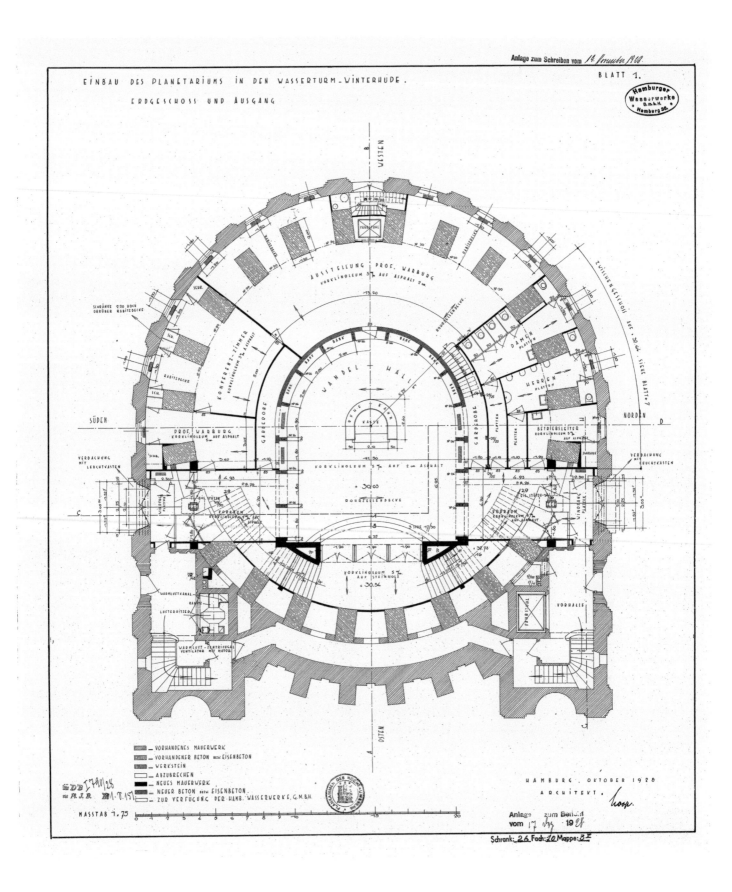

ture into a regular sequence of niches. There were seventeen display stations for the exhibits, chiefly photographic reproductions and plaster casts, largely in chronological order. These related to primitive peoples, Babylonia, and ancient Egypt, followed by Greco-Roman antiquity, and the Arabs and their influence on the Christian world of the Middle Ages and Renaissance, culminating in documents on Albrecht Dürer, Martin Luther, and Johannes Kepler.[7] The material selected by Warburg to show these changing perceptions of the world came together in a rich cycle that would illustrate to visitors "how humanity has tried to interpret and explain the stars and their mysterious movement up to the present."[8]

The exhibition, which opened in 1930, began with a large-format diptych commissioned from Aby's son Max Adolph Warburg.[9] The painting shows the human subject faced with polar concepts of a magical versus a scientific cosmos. It was accompanied by a motto on the wall that revealed the exhibition's wide-ranging didactic ambition: "The history of astronomy shows the diverse forms of the human view of the world. Beginning with fear of demons and with magic, humanity has, always anew, to walk a path towards the abstract logic of scientific observation." The cyclical concept of history that is suggested here ("always anew") should not by any means be understood as desperate, however. After finishing the tour and seeing Kepler oscillate between astrology and astronomy, visitors could breach the fatal loop of the exhibition cycle at precisely that point where it threatened to reimpose itself. Directly beneath the introductory motto that described the ambition of the exhibition, steps rose to the reading room on a mezzanine above. Its study library served the educational goal of the exhibition: to stimulate "self-attained orientation."[10] In this physical climb to the reading room, Warburg dramatized a metaphorical rise to higher knowledge.

The architectural layout and the pedagogical intention of the collection of images were thus very closely connected. The arrangement suggested both a closed cycle (a tour of the exhibition's stations brought visitors back exactly to the point at which they started their journey) and an open trajectory (visitors could leave the closed system of the exhibition proper, escaping like comets into an unfamiliar space of knowledge in the mezzanine library above). The spatial orientation provided by the exhibition thus demands reflection on the philosophy of history, a reflection that applies not only to Warburg's study of astrological and astronomic issues but also to his understanding of the processes of world history in general. A hybrid thinking was displayed here that included cyclical and evolutionary aspects. Visitors could physically trace humanity's path from primitive ideas to the scientific rationality of the modern age. At the same time, some of the exhibits let them experience the simultaneous existence of mythos and logos, the two centres of gravity in Warburg's "elliptical" view of history. At the Planetarium, the orbit this journey involved did not constitute a true ellipse like that found in the famous reading room and lecture hall of his Kulturwissenschaftliche Bibliothek. Yet the geometric form of the exhibition room, with its segmented shape that contrasted an enfolded external wall of early history—primitive peoples and antique symbols—and a smooth inner wall that displayed later periods, was presumably supposed to elicit a comparable bipolar association. Warburg's line of thought and the circular tour of the exhibition were thus interlocked with each other. The floor plan of the *Bildersammlung zur Geschichte von Sternglaube und Sternkunde* was at the same time the plan of a *Denkraum* (thinking-space) that provided cultural-scientific insight. By lending a symbolic form to the exhibition in the Hamburg Planetarium, as he had to the building for his library, Aby Warburg became the architect of a genuine "problem building."[11]

Hans Loop, Floor plan
for the installation of
the Planetarium in the
water tower in Hamburg's
Stadtpark, 1928.

Seesawing
Dag Erik Elgin

One exhibit was missing in the exhibition *Warburg Models at Blaker* in May 2021: the model of the cargo ship *Hermia* that left Hamburg for London on December 12, 1933, evacuating the Kulturwissenschaftliche Bibliothek Warburg (KBW) shortly after the Nazi *Machtergreifung*. The *Hermia* model was complete at the time but had been prevented by physical circumstances from making the journey from London, where it was built, to the exhibition site in Norway. The absence of the model was made present by an empty display table, placed on the balcony outside the exhibition venue's panoramic window. Opening a gap in the exhibition, this empty pedestal provided a view onto a transport network of railroad tracks stretching toward the Norwegian border and the Glomma river flowing toward the sea.

From a visitor's perspective, tracks and river became implicated in the story communicated by the display table's empty black top, forming a suggestive confluent movement between two opposites: an outside world with its logistical contingencies, and the hermetical exhibition situation, where logistics generally only become apparent on the occasion of a hiccup. Given its placement half outdoors on a balcony, the empty display structure became ambiguous in status, oscillating between being part of the exhibition and referencing a prospective model somewhere outside of the defined boundaries of the exhibition space.

As such, this lacuna became a metaphor par excellence, both for the transitory situation and the displacement of Warburg's library that the model sought to capture. The transport infrastructures of the railway tracks and river were "carried across" (Greek: *metapherein*) into the exhibition as doubles of the cargo ship. The displaced display table was a Warburgian image-vehicle: a *Bilderfahrzeug* made manifest; a vessel capable of carrying *Hermia*'s presence in absentia into the exhibition by power of allusion.

According to Henri Bergson, memory denotes not only the recollection of the past in the present but represents a fundamental prerequisite for movement by virtue of its capacity to propel conscious bodies toward the future. Even *hypomnemata*, memories made matter (whether historical architectural models, sculptures, or monuments), appear stable and lasting only insofar as they are carried into the future by constant renegotiation of their meaning in new networks of significance, speculation, and forms of attention. In the context of *Warburg Models at Blaker*, any rigid notion of memory modelled on an unchanging past would be foreign to the KBW, which has continuously generated new social ontologies through encounters with new others.

In a series of largely unpublished drawings that vacillate between handwriting and text, Warburg illustrates precisely this dynamic production of memory in models of his *dynamogram*, the graph capturing the fundamental principles of movement in the production and projection of historical memory.

Several of the drawings found in Warburg's unpublished manuscript "Monistic Psychology of Art" depict a seesaw with an Aesthetician ("Ae") balancing on its hinge, negotiating the forces distributed among two seated figures. (Georges Didi-Huberman was the first to discuss the importance of this seesawing figure to Warburg's systolic and diastolic thinking in *The Surviving Image: Phantoms of Time and Time of Phantoms: Aby Warburg's History of Art* (2017).) These drawings, part figure and part diagram, flow from an identical source: Aby Warburg's fountain pen moving across paper. As thought models, and in their complete self-referentiality, they destabilize the conception of the model as something that refers to something other than itself, capturing contingencies in seismographic registrations of a movement between two opposites. Immaterial forces are glimpsed through clusters of individual pen strokes that materialize as text becoming figure. The precarious balancing act of the Aesthetician embodies a form of knowledge that does not seek to solve or settle contradictions through differentiation between conflicting symptoms, outside and inside, here and now, but constantly remains receptive toward these interdependent forces. The drawings do not model, they *are*. They inscribe the balancing act from which they emerge. They simultaneously "de-pict" and "de-scribe."

It is evident that this Aesthetician, whose centre of gravity is distributed between the contradictions of history, is Warburg himself. The subject appears in the margins of his own text as an "unassailable lacuna that brings to light a lack within the text … or indeed *writes*," adumbrating Michel de Certeau's description of his own appearance in *The Writing of History* (1988). For the Aesthetician balancing in this borderland, the conventionally defined contours between subject and object, personal experience and analytical distance, become blurred. He is rather left to an ocean of material forces and a constant negotiation toward an unknown other. What is at stake is the performative potential of the seesawing figure in the production of a form of immediate and always incomplete knowledge.

Warburg's figure of *The Eternal Seesaw* is the imprint of a stroke of lightning that uncovers an unforeseen connection: an apparatus allowing for continuous movement and meaning production, prospectively capturing a not-yet-known that escapes being modelled in the vernacular sense of the word but, rather, in the moment of drawing, simply *is*.

If the seesaw is the model of an unmodellable absence that encourages writing, then the absence that spurred this short reflection was the missing architectural model of SS *Hermia*. In the 2023-24 exhibition *Warburg Models: Buildings as Bilderfahrzeuge, Hermia* in model form will join the other containers that have housed the Warburg Institute. In conversation with Mara Trübenbach, who designed and built the model, I have closely followed the development and production of an object which, being a vessel, embodies the essence of the KBW. I look forward to the prospect of experiencing this important contribution in the context of the other historical models of the Warburg Library, in London and Hamburg.

Aby Warburg, *Die Ewige Wippe*
(The Eternal Seesaw), from the
manuscript "Fragments on Expression,"
1890 (WIA, III.43.1.1, p. 110).

The Play of Allusion at Woburn Square

Elizabeth Sears

Here a view into the vestibule of the Warburg Institute, more or less as it looked in 1958 when the building opened to the public. In the background: the "Enquiries" desk, where, through the late 1980s, a receptionist sat before a switchboard, fielding calls. In the foreground: a double door surmounted by a wooden lintel bearing a carved and gilded inscription in Greek, "ΜΝΗΜΟΣΥΝΗ" ("memory"), which replicated the inscription, designed by Fritz Schumacher in 1925, incised in stone over the double door in the foyer of the Kulturwissenschaftliche Bibliothek Warburg (KBW) in Hamburg.[1] Embedded in the wall to the right: a neoclassical relief, somewhat weather-worn, showing the nine muses with their defining attributes. These two embellishments and others were owed to the initiative of Gertrud Bing, who in February 1955 (after over thirty years on the staff) had been appointed director of the Institute and Professor of the History of the Classical Tradition at the University of London.[2] Her brief term of office, through her retirement at the end of the academic year 1958-59, coincided with the final design, construction, and outfitting of the Warburg half of the proposed Courtauld-Warburg Building on Woburn Square. In 1955 she wrote to Eric Warburg: "It is a tribute to your uncle that I should have been chosen to carry on his work into another phase, and to see the Institute into the new, bigger home on the main University site, because I am still in the direct line of descent from him."[3] By October 1956, as the building was rising, she could describe a decorative programme to come, listing four items:

"A relief of the Nine Muses in Coade stone after a classical sarcophagus dismantled from the façade of No. 1, Gordon Square will be preserved and let into the entrance wall. Lord Pembroke is very generously prepared to lend a marble statue of Hermes Kriophoros from the collection at Wilton House for an unspecified length of time; and the Hon. Mrs. Bertram Bell has kindly consented to the loan of the famous Jenkins Vase, which will be placed in the entrance to the inner courtyard. A copy of Rembrandt's painting in Stockholm, *The Conspiracy of Claudius Civilis*, which used to hang in the Institute in Hamburg and has since then been hospitably stored by the Rijksmuseum, will shortly arrive from Amsterdam, to be deposited with the Victoria and Albert Museum until the new building is ready to receive it. In its own way each of these four objects illustrates the Institute's concern with the survival of classical art."[4]

1. It must have been startling for Bing to come upon a replica of the front face of the Muses sarcophagus in the Louvre (Roman, second century) set in an exterior wall of the stateliest of the terrace houses slated for demolition to make way for the new Warburg Institute. The act of salvage and reuse—finding ample precedents in "the classical tradition"—would itself have been satisfying. But doubtless making the find appear providential was its relation to Warburg's research. He had incorporated photographs of the object's front and side face among the classical prototypes on Plate 2 of his great work, the never finished pictorial atlas titled *Mnemosyne*.[5] An added nicety: as the mythological Mnemosyne was mother of the muses, the lintel and the relief together invited the visitor to enter a *mouseion*—a centre dedicated to the acquisition of received knowledge and the pursuit of arts of the spirit and intellect.

2. In 1956 Bing approached The Rt. Hon. Lord Herbert, Earl of Pembroke, about a possible loan of two ancient marbles in the family's collection at Wilton House, both of them early imperial Roman works adopting an archaizing Greek style: a votive plaque to Zeus and a statue of Hermes Kriophoros (Hermes the ram-bearer). During a visit the previous summer, when the Institute had been allowed to photograph objects of interest, Bing had noticed these works stored in the stables. Lord Herbert declined to loan the first item (the plaque was by then on exhibit in the house) but agreed that the Institute might borrow the Hermes. Justifying her request, Bing had spoken of the Institute's current interest in classical sculpture that had been "above ground" and known to artists in the Renaissance, noting that the Hermes had been part of the famed mid-seventeenth-century Mazarin Collection.[6] In 1958 Bing described the statue's installation as she thanked the lender.

"I am glad to report that it has found a very dignified place in the entrance hall of our new building where it stands on a plinth against a pillar. You will understand that its presence gives character to what would otherwise be a conventional modern entrance hall, and we are particularly pleased with it since the classical figure, which is the pagan forerunner of the Christian Good Shepherd, tunes in so well with the scope of the Warburg Institute."[7]

3. In 1955 Bing learned from Jacob Hess in Rome—a long-time friend of the Institute then conducting research on the marble "Jenkins Vase"—that its owner, Mrs. Malcolm Bell, was proposing to sell the work or to loan it to an art

Warburg Institute vestibule.
Photo: Pino Guidolotti, 2011.

gallery; at present it was crated up in Marbury Hall in Northwich, Cheshire. Hess having prepared the way, Bing wrote to Mrs. Bell "as a stranger," sending along a brochure about the Warburg Institute and two recent annual reports, making a case for the loan: at the Institute, where it would be seen by many, it would be valued as a "living witness" to the survival of Greek and Roman antiquity, "not only because it is a classical object but also because it was mounted in the 18th century in this country, and therefore shows how much classical art was appreciated here."[8] When Hess's essay came into their hands, the Warburgians learned more about the imposing pastiche, 172 centimetres in height.[9] At its core was a round Roman well-head, known in the Renaissance, that bore a relief carving of the marriage of Paris and Helen. The entrepreneurial British art dealer in Rome, Thomas Jenkins, after acquiring the item, had had a great cup-shaped foot added below and a lip above, circa 1772; shortly thereafter the "vase" was purchased by James Hugh Smith Barry and shipped to England. In 1958 Bing provided the lender with an account of the work's installation.

"I am glad to be able to report that the Jenkins Vase has now found its place in our new building. As you will readily imagine, the transport here was a considerable job and the whole Institute was anxiously and interestedly watching while six men brought the vase through our courtyard and into the building. It now occupies a very good place in one of our Library stack-rooms in front of a big French window looking out onto the courtyard where it is planned to make a garden which I hope, will even have some distinction."[10]

4. In 1925 Warburg commissioned from Carl Schuberth a full-scale copy of Rembrandt's painting *The Conspiracy of the Batavians under Claudius Civilis* (National Museum, Stockholm).[11] The commission was an outcome of Warburg's embrace of a new area of research—a step which persuaded Fritz Saxl, and doubtless Bing, that his cure, after the mental breakdown in 1918, had been effected.[12] They witnessed Warburg make seventeenth-century Dutch verbal, visual, and dramatic culture his own, acquiring leverage for comparison as he applied a longstanding question to the new material: Which elements of the antique heritage so strongly interested Rembrandt's age that they were able to enter as style-shaping artistic forces? In a talk delivered at the KBW on May 29, 1926, Warburg turned his attention to the politically charged cycle adorning the Amsterdam Town Hall for which Rembrandt's painting was intended. The commissioners had chosen as a theme Tacitus's tale of resistance against Roman imperial might on the part of the ancestors of the Dutch. But precisely that which Warburg admired in the painting they could not condone: Rembrandt's darkly sober, monumentalizing rendition of deeply rooted ritual and his distancing resistance to the empty gestural pathos adopted by fellow artists.[13] Schuberth's canvas arrived in Hamburg in December 1926. It hung briefly in the elliptical reading room before being transferred to a stairwell in Warburg's home next door and then, later, transferred back to the library. In 1955 Bing, learning that Warburg's son Max Adolph had had the work shipped to Amsterdam for safekeeping after 1933, proceeded to arrange its homecoming. Initially (so institutional memory has it), wall space was found in the cloakroom on the ground floor.

At another point Bing would have occasion to comment on the titulus ΜΝΗΜΟΣΥΝΗ. A catalogue of the library was published in 1961 and a brief history of the Institute supplied.[14] Having overseen the reinstallation of the holdings on four floors that echoed the arrangements in the purpose-built predecessor in Hamburg, Bing was prepared to offer her sense of the library's logic in relation to "memory."

"The library was to lead from the visual image (*Bild*), as the first stage of man's awareness, to language (*Wort*) and thence to religion, science, and philosophy, all of them products of man's search for orientation (*Orientierung*) which influences his patterns of behaviour and his actions, the subject matter of history. Action, the performance of rites (*drōmena*), in its turn is superseded by reflection which leads back to linguistic formulation and the crystallization of image symbols that complete the cycle. Warburg had come to see in the Mediterranean civilizations the mint of these persistent images which direct and haunt the Western mind. They live on in our civilization much as memory images live on in the individual's mind and it was for this reason that Warburg placed the word ΜΝΕΜΟΣΥΝΕ, memory, over the entrance to his library."[15]

Remodelling the Warburg Institute

Bill Sherman

In English, we have a surfeit of words for work on old buildings—whether we are updating existing spaces or extending the structure in one or more directions. The construction project I inherited when I started my tenure as director of the Warburg Institute (in October 2017) has been described as a "refurbishment" and a "renovation"; but the word that works best for the purposes of this book is "remodelling."

The Warburg Renaissance (as our capital project has been named) is the first full-scale modification of the Institute's permanent home in London since it was built—as Charles Holden's final contribution to the University of London's central Bloomsbury master plan—in the late 1950s. There was a proposal in the 1990s to create new space for the ever-growing library in the empty courtyard, but all that is left of that plan is a partial infill of the void on one façade and a small-scale model preserved in the ground-floor reading room. At that time, new room for books and improved conditions for readers were created by rotating the shelves ninety degrees and installing carpet-covered, under-floor heating. In the intervening years, we have run out of space for books again and the heating system has long since stopped working. Moreover, by running the shelving in parallel (rather than perpendicular) to the outer walls, we have baked the bay of books facing the windows while cutting off the penetration of natural light through the rest of the floor.

A core budget of £9.5 million from the University of London and some £6 million of charitable donations has given us the more than £15 million needed to remodel the Institute in earnest. We began with the problems outlined above and a feasibility study was completed in 2016, identifying a number of necessary repairs—including the leaking roof, the creaking system of fan heaters and obsolete technology for IT and AV. But the project gave us an opportunity to consider the whole architectural history of the Institute and ask not just what Holden had left unfinished but which aspects of the original home in Hamburg had dropped away during the itinerant years in London or failed to take root after the exile to England.

The Warburg Renaissance will restore the Institute's pioneering mixture of discovery, display, and debate, and will open its holdings and expertise to new audiences. It will enhance the Warburg's academic resources and teaching spaces and create new facilities for special collections, exhibitions, and events. The project will not only repair our much-loved but long-neglected building but will create a dramatic new structure in the courtyard, with a greatly expanded lecture theatre (above) and new storage and study spaces (below) for our Archives and Special Collections. The library will be given room to breathe again, with room for twenty to thirty years' growth; and by rotating the shelves and stripping out

The "Great Model" built by
model maker Ellie Sampson,
Haworth Tompkins Architects,
Warburg Renaissance Project,
2019.

the flooring, the original ambience will be restored. The double-height ground floor will be opened to the public for the first time, with the Institute's first gallery for physical and digital display, the permanent installation of Edmund de Waal's *library of exile* and a touch-screen version of Aby Warburg's legendary *Bilderatlas*.

It is no exaggeration to say that our choice of Haworth Tompkins as the architects for the project was influenced by their approach to models. Their proposal for the 2018 competition featured a wide range of graphic modellings that opened our eyes to possible changes. Their initial work on the existing spaces and uses was worked out in 3D (both on site and in their studio), and the shape and function of the new structure in the courtyard was debated with the help of a model showing the entire outside of the building. By the time we settled on the current design—far larger than the original plans and invoking Warburg's elliptical roof from the reading room in Hamburg—the firm's master model-maker, Ellie Sampson, had built an extremely accurate 1:25 representation, complete with interior walls and furnishings, that could be used for solving spatial problems and for creating atmospheric photographs. These, rather than generic CGIs or computerized fly-throughs, have conveyed the vision of the prospective project to potential funders and the members of our internal and external steering groups. And thanks to the work of Tim Anstey, Mari Lending, and their students in Oslo, models of various kinds have allowed us to travel back in time and revisit the buildings occupied by the Institute in the past.

As a practice, Haworth Tompkins is best known for its playhouses and concert halls. While the Warburg Renaissance has more in common with the firm's work on the London Library, the Victoria and Albert Museum's Clothworkers' Centre, and new buildings for the Royal College of Art and Kingston School of Art, Sampson's model turned our building into a miniature theatre where architects and clients alike could act out different stories and scenarios. And during the nearly two years it will take for the project to play out, the model (now on display in the front of our reading room) allows us to visit the building as it will be once the remodelling is complete. Architectural models have, in other words, served as the vehicles for joining past, present, and future—proving themselves to be Warburgian instruments of the highest order.

Ernst Kitzinger at work in the reading room, Thames House, ca. 1935–36.

WARBURG MODEL DETAILS

Kulturwissenschaftliche Bibliothek Warburg

Hamburg Planetarium

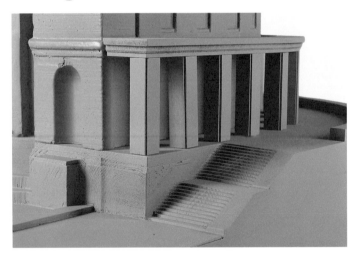

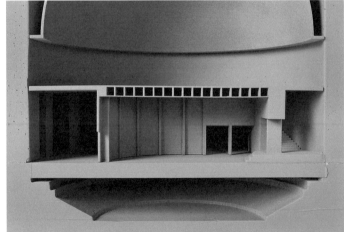

Thames House

Cottage at Bromley

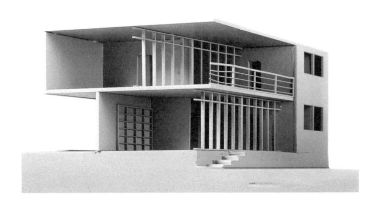
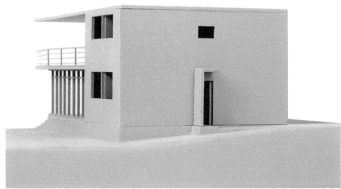

Imperial Institute

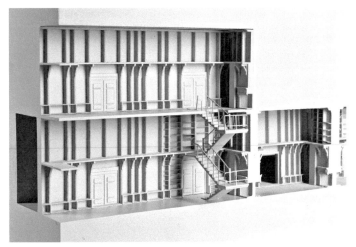

Woburn Square

NOTES

WARBURG MODELS

1 Fritz Saxl, "The History of Warburg's Library (1886-1944)," a memoir drafted around 1943, published as an appendix to Ernst Gombrich, *Aby Warburg: An Intellectual Biography* (London, 1970), p. 332.

2 Ibid., p. 327.

3 Ibid., p. 332.

4 Ibid., p. 334.

5 Eric M. Warburg, "The Transfer of the Institute to England," appendix to the *Warburg Institute Annual Report 1952-1953* (London, 1953), p. 13.

6 Herbert Weisinger, "The Warburg Institute," unpublished paper delivered to the Modern Language Association, 1962, Warburg Institute Library, NBM 80.

7 Sydney Anglo, "From South Kensington to Bloomsbury and Beyond," in *Vorträge aus dem Warburg-Haus: The Afterlife of the Kulturwissenschaftliche Bibliothek Warburg*, edited by Uwe Fleckner and Peter Mack (Berlin, 2015), pp. 65-70, at 66.

8 *The Warburg Institute Annual Report, 1951-1952* (London, 1952), p. 1.

9 Saxl, in Gombrich 1970 (see note 1), p. 331.

10 Aby Warburg to the KBW, March 26, 1929, transcribed in Uwe Fleckner et al., *Aby M. Warburg: Bildersammlung zur Geschichte von Sternglaube und Sternkunde im Hamburger Planetarium* (Hamburg, 1993), p. 66.

11 "It is common ground that the new Building should be low in height and have not more than 4 floors in all: (1) Basement, (2) Ground floor, (3) First floor, (4) Top-lit Gallery above. The general architectural style of the building should, (mutatis mutandis) conform in spirit to that of its 'parent' institution, the 'Fogg Museum of Art' at Harvard University.... The material to be red brick with stone dressings." Warburg Institute Archive (WIA), I.7.1.2, "Memorandum for the Building Sub-Committee—New Courtauld-Warburg Building," undated copy, almost certainly from 1945.

12 Saxl, in Gombrich 1970 (see note 1), p. 331.

BUILDINGS AS BILDERFAHRZEUGE

1 On the Hamburg Planetarium, see Uwe Fleckner et al., *Aby M. Warburg: Bildersammlung zur Geschichte von Sternglaube und Sternkunde im Hamburger Planetarium* (Hamburg, 1993).

2 Aby Warburg to Ernst Cassirer, September 6, 1928, London, Warburg Institute Archive (WIA), General Correspondence (GC).

3 Fleckner 1993 (see note 1), pp. 250-79.

4 Ibid., pp. 119, 123.

5 Aby Warburg, "Italienische Kunst und internationale Astrologie im Palazzo Schifanoia zu Ferrara," in Adolfo Venturi, ed., *L'Italia e l'Arte straniera: Atti del X Congresso Internazionale di Storia dell'Arte in Roma* (Rome, 1922), pp. 179-93.

6 Aby Warburg, "Italian Art and International Astrology in the Palazzo Schifanoia, Ferrara," in *The Renewal of Pagan Antiquity: Contributions to the Cultural History of the European Renaissance*, trans. David Britt, with an introduction by Kurt W. Forster (Los Angeles, 1999), p. 565.

7 Warburg's analysis of the frescoes, and Warburg and Saxl's respective contributions to the history of astrology in art, are interrogated by Kristen Lippincott, "Urania Redux: An Overview of Aby Warburg's Writings on Art and Astrology," in Richard Woodfield, ed., *Art History as Cultural History: Warburg's Projects* (Amsterdam, 2001), pp. 160-64. Lippincott notes limitations in Warburg's analysis.

8 Warburg 1999 (see note 6), p. 573.

9 Ibid., p. 573.

10 Ibid., pp. 567-72.

11 Ibid., pp. 567-72.

12 Ibid., p. 572.

13 Ibid., p. 566.

14 All three exemplars inform the panels of the *Bilderatlas*, where images of the Schifanoia frescoes are disposed in series from right to left, as they are within the actual architecture of the room, on panel 27; where the *salone* in Padua and its interpretation occupy panel 23; and where the Mithraeum is included on panel 8. *Aby Warburg: Bilderatlas Mnemosyne; The Original*, ed. Roberto Ohrt and Axel Heil (Berlin and London, 2020).

15 Aby Warburg to the Kulturwissenschaftliche Bibliothek Warburg (KBW), March 26, 1929; Fritz Saxl to Aby Warburg, April 12, 1929; Fritz Saxl to Fritz Schumacher, November 21, 1929, WIA, GC; all transcribed in Fleckner 1993 (see note 1), pp. 65-75.

16 Aby Warburg to Felix von Eckardt, October 3, 1928, Hamburger Staatsarchiv, Bestand Staatliche Pressestelle I–IV, no. 5061; transcribed in Fleckner 1993 (see note 1), pp. 58–59.

17 Warburg 1999 (see note 6), p. 564.

18 Warburg described his reaction to Lippi in his 1927 presentation of the aims of the KBW, "Vom Arsenal zum Laboratorium." Aby Warburg, "From the Arsenal to the Laboratory," trans. Christopher Johnson, annot. Claudia Wedepohl, *West 86th* 19, no. 1, 2012: 114. On Warburg's trip to Florence in 1888-89, see Claudia Wedepohl, "Why Botticelli? Aby Warburg's Search for a New Approach to Quattrocento Italian Art," in Ana Debenedetti and Caroline Elam, eds., *Botticelli Past and Present* (London, 2019), pp. 192-94.

19 Ludwig Binswanger, "Histoire clinique [d'Aby Warburg]," 1921-24, in *La Guérison infinie: Histoire clinique d'Aby Warburg*, ed. Davide Stimilli, trans. Maël Renouard and Martin Rueff (Paris, 2007), pp. 53-180.

20 Aby Warburg, "Airship and Submarine in the Medieval Imagination," in Warburg 1999 (see note 6), pp. 333-37.

21 The domestic nature of the spaces in the first schemes for the KBW can be seen in the architectural drawings by Felix Ascher. Felix Ascher, "Plans and section, Bibliothek Warburg," 1924, WIA, I.3.1, Warburg Institute, University of London.

22 On the building process, see Tilmann von Stockhausen, *Die Kulturwissenschaftliche Bibliothek Warburg: Architektur, Einrichtung und Organisation* (Hamburg, 1992), pp. 42-52.

23 On the move, see Elizabeth Sears, "The Warburg Institute, 1933-1944: A Precarious Experiment in International Collaboration," *Art Libraries Journal* 38, no. 4, 2013: 6-7. The list of chattels transported is given by Fritz Saxl, "The Warburg Institute: Gift to London University," *Manchester Guardian*, December 13, 1944, p. 4.

24 G. A. Harvey & Co. (London) to Fritz Saxl, January 6, 1934, Godfrey Samuel Papers, Series 2: Projects undertaken by Samuel, 1933-38, RIBA Drawings Collection, Victoria and Albert Museum, London.

25 Two architectural drawings are preserved in the Warburg Institute Archive that show early plan variants for the library at Thames House. One is marked up for pricing electrical works, based on the initial architectural scheme, WIA, I.5.5.3; the other is a plan of the ground floor of the whole building, showing a first sketch layout for the Warburg Institute occupancy, WIA, I.5.5.1. On both the chamfered corners proposed for the reading room are clearly shown; the first plan notes that "Tenants shelving and tables" will occupy the reading room, and these are shown with a similar dotted line. Photographs of the completed project confirm that the perimeter shelving and readers' tables coincide with the furniture used in Hamburg.

26 A drawing for the epidiascope rostrum, "Lantern Stand for the Warburg Library," and a sketch of the installation requirements are preserved in the Godfrey Samuel Papers, 1933-38 (see note 24).

27 The fittings are clearly visible in photographs commissioned by the Institute relating to the interiors at Thames House and the Imperial Institute: WIA, I.5.1, photograph of book stacks at Thames House; WIA, I.6.2, photograph of book stacks at the Imperial Institute Buildings. The fittings at Thames House are described in letters between Godfrey Samuel and the electrical suppliers Luxfer, February 10, 1934, Godfrey Samuel Papers, 1933-38 (see note 24).

28 Adams Holden & Pearson, Warburg Institute, University of London, Schedule B: Existing furniture to be reused in the new building, November 1957, WIA, I.7.7.2.

29 Gertrud Bing to Kenneth Urquhart, Adams Holden & Pearson, March 18, 1955, WIA, GC. See also Adams Holden & Pearson, Warburg Institute, University of London, Floor plans: Basement to Fourth floor, showing arrangement of furniture, drawing nos. LU 7748-7753, Rev E, after February 7, 1957, WIA, I.7.3.

30 Fritz Saxl, "Needs of the Warburg Institute in Connection with the Projected New Building for the Courtauld and Warburg Institutes," June 22, 1945, WIA, I.7.1.1.

31 Deliberations about the construction of the Mnemosyne inscription occupied letters between Gertrud Bing and Kenneth Urquhart during December 1957. Kenneth C. Urquhart to Gertrud Bing, December 17, 1957, WIA, GC; Preliminary Sketches "New Building," Subsection "Details 1955-59," WIA, I.1.7.

32 Correspondence between Godfrey Samuel and H.C. Slingsby First International Truck Builder, February 15, 20, and March 7, 1934, Godfrey Samuel Papers, 1933-38 (see note 24).

33 Saxl 1945 (see note 30).

34 The correspondence, sketches, and drawings are contained in the Godfrey Samuel Papers, 1933-38 (see note 24).

35 Donald Gordon, "In Memoriam Gertrud Bing," in Ernst Gombrich, ed., *In Memoriam Gertrud Bing: 1892-1964* (London, 1965), p. 17.

36 Ibid., p. 22.

BUILDING BIOGRAPHIES

Kulturwissenschaftliche Bibliothek Warburg, 1924–33

1 Felix Ascher, "Plans and Section, Bibliothek Warburg," 1924. Warburg Institute Archive (WIA), I.3.1.

2 Gerhard Langmaack, Kulturwissenschaftliche Bibliothek Warburg (KBW), longitudinal section, autograph annotations by Aby Warburg, ca. 1926, WIA, I.4.8.1.

3 Gertrud Bing, Autograph notes on positioning of library subject headings, KBW, ca. 1926, WIA, I.4.17.

4 Gerhard Langmaack, Presentation Album, KBW, 1926, WIA, I.4.20.3.

5 "Projektplan Gerhard Langmaack: Neubau Kulturwissenschaftliche Bibliothek Warburg, Hamburg," Section 5, *Die technischen Einzelheiten*, part o., transcribed in Tilmann von Stockhausen, *Die Kulturwissenschaftliche Bibliothek Warburg: Architektur, Einrichtung und Organisation* (Hamburg, 1992), pp. 141-43. Wolf Netter & Jacobi also produced steel card-index boxes, trolleys, book stands, and ladders; see *Regale aus Stahl*, undated product catalogue, ca. 1925, Wolf Netter & Jacobi Collection, The Leo Baeck Institute Center for Jewish History, New York, AR7212, box 1/1.

6 Gertrud Bing, entry April 29, 1927, in Aby Warburg et al., *Tagebuch der Kulturwissenschaftlichen Bibliothek Warburg* (Berlin, 2001), vol. 2, p. 123.

Hamburg Planetarium, 1927–30

1 On the Planetarium project, see Uwe Fleckner et al., *Aby M. Warburg: Bildersammlung zur Geschichte von Sternglaube und Sternkunde im Hamburger Planetarium* (Hamburg, 1993).

2 Charles E. Closmann, "Chaos and Contamination: Water Pollution and Economic Upheaval in Hamburg, 1919-1923," *Journal of Urban History* 33, no. 5 (July 2007): 838.

3 Aby Warburg to Felix von Eckardt, October 3, 1928, Hamburger Staatsarchiv, Bestand Staatliche Pressestelle I-IV, no. 5061; printed in Fleckner 1993 (see note 7), pp. 58-59.

4 Aby Warburg to Ernst Zinn, April 1, 1929; Karl Umlauf to Aby Warburg, April 23, 1929; Emil Krause to Max Warburg, August 7, 1929; Max Warburg to Emil Krause, August 8, 1929; Georg Thilenius to Governor von Wrochem, November 13, 1929. The correspondence is transcribed in Fleckner 1993 (see note 7), pp. 66-74.

5 Aby Warburg to Felix von Eckardt, October 3, 1928; Karl Umlauf to Aby Warburg, October 10, 1928; Aby Warburg to Karl Umlauf, October 13, 1928; Karl Umlauf to Aby Warburg, April 23, 1929. Ibid., pp. 58-61.

6 Uwe Fleckner, "From the Mythical to Mathematical Orientation: The 'Cosmologicon' of the Hamburg Planetarium as a Branch of the Kulturwissenschaftliche Bibliothek Warburg," *ARJ. Art Research Journal* 9, no. 1 (2022): 2-4.

Thames House, 1934–37

1 John Allan, *Berthold Lubetkin: Architecture and the Tradition of Progress* (London, 1992).

2 Elizabeth Sears, "The Warburg Institute, 1933-1944: A Precarious Experiment in International Collaboration," *Art Libraries Journal* 38, no. 4, 2013: 8.

3 "Layout of the Warburg Institute at Thames House," Tecton Drawings, RIBA Drawings Collection, Victoria and Albert Museum, London.

4 Godfrey Samuel, "Lantern Stand for the Warburg Library, Thames House," 1934. Ibid.

5 Gertrud Bing, "The Warburg Institute," *Library Association Record* 35, no. 4 (August 1934): 265.

BUILDING BIOGRAPHIES (cont.)

Cottage at Bromley, 1934–35 (unbuilt)

1 Godfrey Samuel to Gertrud Bing, January 1, 1935. Godfrey Samuel Papers, Series 2: Projects undertaken by Samuel, 1933-38, RIBA Drawings Collection, Victoria and Albert Museum, London. An itemized list of changes to the project includes: "3. More room for furniture in Living Rooms, (but I think it may be necessary for some of Dr. Saxl's furniture to be used by you); 4. Internal access to the heating chamber from your kitchen; 5. Basement storage for unwanted furniture. (Note: the following pieces of furniture have not been included—Saxl, 9, 10, 23 and 38: Bing 13.) ... I am returning the schedule of furniture at the same time so that you can identify the pieces in the plan."

2 Donald Gordon, "In Memoriam Gertrud Bing," in Ernst Gombrich, ed., *In Memoriam Gertrud Bing: 1892-1964* (London, 1965), p. 11.

3 Michael Baxandall, *Episodes: A Memory Book* (London, 2010), p. 114.

4 Gordon 1965 (see note 2), p. 16.

Imperial Institute Buildings, 1937–59

1 *The Warburg Institute Annual Report 1937-1938* (London, 1938), WIA, Ia.2.5. A typewritten document including Gertrud Bing's description of the arrangement of the Warburg Library in the Imperial Institute Buildings (pp. 1-7), dated February 16, 1938, gives room three as "Dr. Wittkower's room," while room four "is the one to be occupied by Mr. Blunt." WIA, Ia.2.5, pp. 1-4.

2 Ibid., pp. 4-6.

3 *The Warburg Institute Annual Report 1949-1950* (London, 1950), pp. 1-2.

4 Ibid., p. 65.

5 In the report the contents of the library is described in the order "I. Orientation by means of myth, magic and logic; II. The Word as the vehicle of expression and tradition; III. The Image as the vehicle of expression; IV. The significant Act (*Dromenon*). *Warburg Institute Annual Report 1951-1952* (London, 1952), p. 1.

Woburn Square, 1958

1 Douglas William Logan, "Memorandum for the Warburg Institute Committee of Management March 4, 1954, from the Principal [of the University]," WIA, I.1.7.2.

2 A developed scheme for the Warburg and Courtauld Institute located at the corner of Torrington Place and Gordon Square and Woburn Square, requested by the principal of the University at a Building Sub-Committee meeting on February 8, 1954, was exhibited at the Imperial Institute Buildings after March 1954. Revised drawings of the Warburg Institute only, with a reduced footprint, were presented at a Building Sub-Committee meeting on August 12, 1954. The detailed scheme-design was finalized by June 1955. WIA, I.7.3, Minutes of the Building Sub-Committee.

3 WIA, I.7.1.2, "Memorandum for the Building Sub-Committee—New Courtauld-Warburg Building," undated copy, almost certainly from 1945.

4 Adams Holden & Pearson, Elevational and Sectional Studies for a New Building for the Courtauld and Warburg Institutes, ca. 1945, RIBA Drawings Collection. Adams Holden & Pearson, Designs for the Warburg Institute, Woburn Square.

5 Fritz Saxl, "Needs of the Warburg Institute in connection with the projected New Building for the Courtauld and Warburg Institutes," June 22, 1945, WIA, I.7.1.1.

6 "I have set out how I have reached a total of approximately 17,000 square feet, required for placing the library, as we wish it, undivided on one floor." Henri Frankfort, "Revised Schedule of Accommodation for the Warburg Institute," June 16, 1953, WIA, I.7.1.1.

7 W. Fankl to Gertrud Bing, March 15, 1953, WIA, GC.

8 Gertrud Bing to Raymond Klibansky, April 25, 1958. Deutsches Literaturarchiv Marbach A: Klibansky, pp. XX–XXI, 1.

TRIANGULATIONS

The Elliptical Reading Room as Denkraum

1 Ludwig Binswanger and Aby Warburg, *Die unendliche Heilung: Aby Warburgs Krankengeschichte*, ed. Davide Stimilli and Chantal Marazia (Zurich and Berlin, 2007).

2 The first to record the symbolic meaning were Fritz Saxl, "Ernst Cassirer," in Paul Arthur Schilpp, ed., *The Philosophy of Ernst Cassirer* (Evanston, IL, 1949), pp. 47-51, at 50; and Fritz Schumacher, "Aby Warburg und seine Bibliothek" (1949), in Stefan Füssel, ed., *Mnemosyne: Beiträge zum 50. Todestag von Aby M. Warburg* (Göttingen, 1979), pp. 42-46, at 44. Based on Schumacher's memories, Martin Jesinghausen-Lauster, *Die Suche nach der symbolischen Form: Der Kreis um die Kulturwissenschaftliche Bibliothek Warburg* (Baden-Baden, 1985), p. 198, concludes that the form and content of the KBW represented an allegory of macrocosm (i.e., the universe) and microcosm (i.e., the human body). Tilmann von Stockhausen, in *Die Kulturwissenschaftliche Bibliothek Warburg: Architektur, Einrichtung und Organisation* (Hamburg, 1992), pp. 37-39, points to Ernst Cassirer's role in finding the "symbolic form," and associations with electricity and the solar system; he describes how the dipolar tension was intended to "energize" its users and how Warburg perceived the atmosphere created. The full story is reconstructed in Horst Bredekamp and Claudia Wedepohl, *Warburg, Cassirer und Einstein im Gespräch: Kepler als Schlüssel der Moderne* (Berlin, 2015).

3 Aby Warburg, "Italienische Kunst und internationale Astrologie im Palazzo Schifanoja zu Ferrara," in *Die Erneuerung der heidnischen Antike: Kulturwissenschaftliche Beiträge zur Geschichte der Europäischen Renaissance*, ed. Gertrud Bing (Leipzig and Berlin, 1932), vol. 2, pp. 459-81.

4 Aby Warburg, "I costumi teatrali per gli intermezzi del 1589: i disegni di Bernardino Buontalenti e il libro di conti di Emilio de' Cavalieri" (1895), in Warburg 1932 (see note 3), vol. 1, pp. 259-300.

5 Ernst Cassirer, "Worte zur Beisetzung von Professor Dr. Aby M. Warburg," in Füssel 1979 (see note 2), pp. 15–22, at 17.

6 Claudia Wedepohl, "Einschwingen—Ausschwingen: Oscillation of the Pendulum," in Katia Mazzucco and Beatrice Paolozzi Strozzi, eds., *Lessico Warburghiano: I prestiti della scienze negli scitti d'arte di Aby Warburg*, Accademia Toscana di Scienze e Lettere "La Colombaria," Classe di Scienze storiche e filosofiche 9 (Florence, 2023), pp. 99-131.

7 For Schumacher's plans of December 1924, see Stockhausen 1992 (see note 2), pp. 52-57; for Langmaack's drafts, see pp. 67-74. See also Füssel 1979 (see note 2), p. 302; Hans-Michael Schäfer, *Die Kulturwissenschaftliche Bibliothek Warburg: Geschichte und Persönlichkeiten der Bibliothek Warburg mit Berücksichtigung der Bibliothekenlandschaft und der Stadtsituation der Freien und Hansestadt Hamburg zu Beginn des 20. Jahrhunderts* (Berlin, 2003), pp. 210-20.

8 Stockhausen 1992 (see note 2), p. 102.

TRIANGULATIONS

The Hamburg Planetarium as a Problem Building

1 See Claudia Wedepohl, "Ideengeographie: Ein Versuch zu Aby Warburgs 'Wanderstrassen der Kultur,'" in *Entgrenzte Räume: Kulturelle Transfers um 1900 und in der Gegenwart*, ed. Helga Mitterbauer and Katharina Scherke, Studien zur Moderne 22 (Vienna, 2005), pp. 227-54; Dorothea McEwan, "Aby Warburg's (1866-1929) Dots and Lines: Mapping the Diffusion of Astrological Motifs in Art History," *German Studies Review* 29, no. 2 (2006): 243-68; *Lightning Symbol and Snake Dance: Aby Warburg and Pueblo Art*, ed. Christine Chávez and Uwe Fleckner, exh. cat. Museum am Rothenbaum: Kulturen und Künste der Welt (Hamburg, 2022), pp. 28ff. (cat. nos. 9-12).

2 Aby Warburg to Karl Umlauf, October 13, 1928, in Uwe Fleckner et al., *Aby M. Warburg: Bildersammlung zur Geschichte von Sternglaube und Sternkunde im Hamburger Planetarium* (Hamburg, 1993), p. 61. See Uwe Fleckner, "'... von kultischer Praktik zur mathematischen Kontemplation—und zurück': Aby Warburgs Bildersammlung zur Geschichte von Sternglaube und Sternkunde im Hamburger Planetarium," in Horst Bredekamp, Michael Diers, and Charlotte Schoell-Glass, eds., *Akten des internationalen Aby Warburg-Symposions Hamburg 1990* (Weinheim, 1991), pp. 313-34; Uwe Fleckner, "De la orientación mítica a la matemática: El 'Kosmologikon' del Planetario de Hamburgo como filial en el campo de la educación popular de la Biblioteca Warburg de Ciencias de la Cultura," in *Aby Warburg y el poder de las imágenes: En lucha por el espacio del pensamiento*, trans. Felisa Santos (Buenos Aires, 2020), pp. 164-91; Kohei Suzuki, "'... den Ruach in den Maschinenkloss bringen': Aby Warburg und das Zeiss-Planetarium," in Boris Goesl, Hans-Christian von Herrmann, and Kohei Suzuki, eds., *Zum Planetarium: Wissensgeschichtliche Studien* (Leiden, 2018), pp. 265-307.

3 Aby Warburg to Felix von Eckardt, October 3, 1928, in Fleckner 1993 (see note 2), p. 59.

4 Ibid., p. 58.

5 Aby Warburg to Ernst Cassirer, September 6, 1928, London, Warburg Institute Archive, General Correspondence.

6 See Uwe Fleckner, "Warburg als Erzieher: Bemerkungen zu einem 'Erziehungsmittel für Gebildete und Ungebildete,'" in Fleckner 1993 (see note 2), pp. 316-41; Uwe Fleckner, "Bildersammlung zur Geschichte von Sternglaube und Sternkunde [Kommentar]," in Aby Warburg, *Bilderreihen und Ausstellungen*, ed. Uwe Fleckner and Isabella Woldt (Berlin, 2012), pp. 389-95.

7 See Uwe Fleckner, "La valeur éducative des reproductions photographiques: La 'Collection d'images sur l'histoire de l'astrologie et de l'astronomie' d'Aby Warburg au planétarium de Hambourg," *Transbordeur: Photographie, histoire, société* 2 (2018): pp. 78-91.

8 Gertrud Bing and Fritz Saxl, "Die Bildersammlung zur Geschichte von Sternglaube und Sternkunde," in *Planetarium: Ein Führer* (Hamburg, 1930), p. 16.

9 See Warburg 2012 (see note 6), pp. 400-401 (13.1a-b).

10 Bing and Saxl 1930 (see note 8), p. 19. See Uwe Fleckner, "Die Bibliothek im Hamburger Planetarium," in Fleckner 1993 (see note 2), pp. 308-14; Warburg 2012 (see note 6), pp. 454ff. On the Kepler display wall, see Warburg 2012 (see note 6), pp. 452-53 (17.1-3); Alexander Honold, "Mars regiert: Aby Warburg und das Planetarium des Krieges," in Uwe Fleckner et al., eds., *Vorträge aus dem Warburg-Haus*, vol. 15 (Hamburg, 2021), pp. 53-76.

11 Fritz Saxl, "Die Kulturwissenschaftliche Bibliothek Warburg in Hamburg" (1930), in Aby M. Warburg, *Ausgewählte Schriften und Würdigungen*, ed. Dieter Wuttke, Saecula spiritalia 1 (Baden-Baden, 1979), p. 334 (Saxl used this term for the KBW building).

TRIANGULATIONS

The Play of Allusion at Woburn Square

1 Fritz Schumacher to Aby Warburg, August 11, 1925, Warburg Institute Archive (WIA), General Correspondence (GC). See Uwe Fleckner, "Under the Protection of Mnemosyne: Fritz Schumacher's Drawing for the K. B. W. Lintel Rediscovered," www.warburg.sas.ac.uk/blog/protection-mnemosyne (accessed May 16, 2023).

2 *The Warburg Institute Annual Report 1954-1955* (London, 1955), p. 1.

3 Gertrud Bing to Eric Warburg, February 22, 1955, WIA, Gertrud Bing Papers.

4 *The Warburg Institute Annual Report 1955-1956* (London, 1956), p. 1.

5 *Aby Warburg: Bilderatlas Mnemosyne; The Original*, ed. Roberto Ohrt and Axel Heil (Berlin and London, 2020), pl. 2 ("Greek conception of the cosmos. Mythological figures in the heavens. Apollo. Muses as companions of Apollo"), pp. 32-33.

6 Gertrud Bing to Lord Herbert, February 15, 1956; and reply, February 17, WIA, GC.

7 Gertrud Bing to Lord Herbert, July 31, 1958, WIA, GC. For the return of the statue to Wilton House, see the *Warburg Institute Annual Report 2006-2007* (London, 2007), p. 4.

8 Gertrud Bing to Mrs. Bertram (Dorothy) Bell, December 9, 1955; with copy of Bell to Hess, August 20, 1955, WIA, GC.

9 Jacob Hess, "Amaduzzi und Jenkins in Villa Giulia," *English Miscellany* 6 (1955): 175-204, at 200-204.

10 Gertrud Bing to Mrs. Bell, July 31, 1958, WIA, GC. In 1976 the Jenkins Vase was acquired by the National Museum of Wales (NMW A 14).

11 For a history of the copy across the decades, see Claudia Wedepohl, "Conspiracy in the Common Room," *The Warburg Institute Newsletter*, online edition, 15 (Summer 2004).

12 Fritz Saxl to Paul Warburg, August 5, 1926, in Dorothea McEwan, ed., *Fritz Saxl. Eine Biographie* (Cologne, 2012), pp. 251-53.

13 See Aby Warburg, "Italienische Antike im Zeitalter Rembrandts," 1926, in Pablo Schneider, ed., *Nachhall der Antike: Aby Warburg; Zwei Untersuchungen* (Zurich, 2012), pp. 69-101, with commentary.

14 *The Warburg Institute Annual Report 1957-1958* (London, 1958), p. 1.

15 Gertrud Bing, "Historical Note," *Catalog of the Warburg Institute Library, University of London* (Boston, 1961), front matter.

COLOPHON AND CREDITS

Editors Tim Anstey and Mari Lending
Project management Fabian Reichel
Copyediting Bill Roberts
Translations Steven Lindberg
Graphic design Benedikt Reichenbach
Production Alise Ausmane
Reproductions Schwabenrepro, Fellbach
Printing Livonia Print, Riga
Paper Munken Lynx, 150 g/m²

© 2023 Hatje Cantz Verlag, Berlin, and authors

© 2023 for the reproduced images: the institutions and photographers
according to Illustration credits

Cover: Scale model of the Kulturwissenschaftliche Bibliothek
Warburg by Nora Kilstad and Cathrine Tønseth Sundem (2021),
superimposed on a plan for the the ellipse in the library
by Gerhard Langmaack (1926). Background derived from the
colour chart for coding book spines at the Warburg Library
(1922–81).

Published by
Hatje Cantz Verlag GmbH
Mommsenstrasse 27
10629 Berlin
www.hatjecantz.com
A Ganske Publishing Group Company

ISBN 978-3-7757-5520-7

Printed in Latvia

**Models and drawings by students in the Warburg
Models seminars, AHO, 2020–21**
Pernille Boye Ahlgren, Christian Tømmeraas Berg,
Amalie Elvegård Utigård, Nora Kilstad, Anne Lise Ladegård,
Pål Luis Sanchez-Paredes, Silje Ekornrud Seim,
Cathrine Tønseth Sundem, Maximilian Svendsen,
Karina Tang, Mara Trübenbach.

Illustration Credits
Archive Nicholas Chinardet: p. 51
Archive ouvert HAL: p. 47 (top)
Archive Uwe Fleckner: pp. 20, 23, 27, 43, 44
Christian Tømmeraas, photographer: pp. 42, 52, 56, 60, 82, 83
Flensburger Schifffahrtsmuseum: p. 47 (bottom)
Hamburgisches Architekturarchiv: Cover and pp. 1, 66, 70
Haworth Tompkins Architects: p. 78
Richard Hornsey: p. 13
Royal Institute of British Architects (RIBA): pp. 31 (right),
35, 53, 54, 55
Warburg Institute Archive: pp. 4, 6, 8, 14, 15, 16, 28 (bottom),
30, 31 (left), 33, 39, 40, 41, 47 (middle), 49, 50, 57, 58, 61, 62,
63, 73, 80
Wikipedia Commons: pp. 10, 24, 28 (top), 59